INSIGHT ⊙ GUIDES

ATHENS

POCKET GUIDE

◉ Walking Eye App

YOUR FREE EBOOK AVAILABLE THROUGH THE WALKING EYE APP

Your guide now includes a free eBook to your chosen destination,
for the same great price as before. Simply download the Walking Eye
App from the App Store or Google Play to access your free eBook.

HOW THE WALKING EYE APP WORKS

Through the Walking Eye App, you can purchase a range of eBooks and destination
content. However, when you buy this book, you can download the corresponding
eBook for free. Just see below in the grey panel where to find your free content and
then scan the QR code at the bottom of this page.

Destinations: Download essential destination
content featuring recommended sights and
attractions, restaurants, hotels and an A–Z of
practical information, all available for purchase.

Ships: Interested in ship reviews? Find independent reviews of river and ocean ships in this
section, all available for purchase.

eBooks: You can download your free accom-
panying digital version of this guide here. You
will also find a whole range of other eBooks,
all available for purchase.

Free access to travel-related blog articles
about different destinations, updated on a
daily basis.

HOW THE EBOOKS WORK

The eBooks are provided in EPUB file format. Please note that you will need an eBook reader installed on your device to open the file. Many devices come with this as standard, but you may still need to install one manually from Google Play.

The eBook content is identical to the content in the printed guide.

HOW TO DOWNLOAD THE WALKING EYE APP

1. Download the Walking Eye App from the App Store or Google Play.
2. Open the app and select the scanning function from the main menu.
3. Scan the QR code on this page – you will then be asked a security question to verify ownership of the book.
4. Once this has been verified, you will see your eBook in the purchased ebook section, where you will be able to download it.

Other destination apps and eBooks are available for purchase separately or are free with the purchase of the Insight Guide book.

TOP 10 ATTRACTIONS

NEW ACROPOLIS MUSEUM
A splendid repository for the antiquities of the Acropolis, with space for the Elgin Marbles. See page 39.

BENAKI MUSEUM PIREÓS ANNEXE
Multiple changing exhibits, always top-notch. See page 56.

THE MUSEUM OF CYCLADIC ART
See how modern these delightful ancient sculptures seem. See page 66.

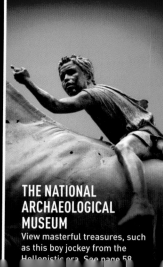

THE NATIONAL ARCHAEOLOGICAL MUSEUM
View masterful treasures, such as this boy jockey from the Hellenistic era. See page 58.

THE ACROPOLIS
Topped by one of the world's greatest cultural monuments, the Parthenon, this is the rock on which ancient Athens was founded. See page 29.

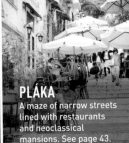

PLÁKA
A maze of narrow streets lined with restaurants and neoclassical mansions. See page 43.

THE ATHENS AND EPIDAUROS FESTIVAL
Especially on a moonlit night, a performance at Herodes Atticus or Epidauros is magical. See page 84.

DELPHI
Make an excursion to the ancient home of the oracle. See page 80.

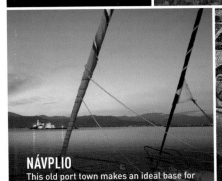

NÁVPLIO
This old port town makes an ideal base for exploring the Argolid. See page 80.

THE BYZANTINE AND CHRISTIAN MUSEUM
Cutting-edge museumology shows unexpected artefacts to advantage. See page 67.

A PERFECT TOUR

Day 1

Acropolis and around

Visit the Acropolis before the crowds. Descend via Pláka, stopping at Kanellopoulos, a low-key local museum. Lunch around Monastiráki. Time it so you arrive at the New Acropolis Museum late in the afternoon, with the Parthenon catching the setting sun while you admire the pediments on the top floor. Treat yourself to an upmarket supper at Edodi.

Day 2

Kolonáki museums

From Evangelismós metro station the Museum of Cycladic Art and the Byzantine and Christian Museum are both just a short walk away, as is the National Gallery – all enhanced by temporary exhibitions. After lunch (and perhaps a spot of shopping) in Kolonáki, visit the Benaki Museum. Pangráti neighbourhood is a likely destination for dinner.

Day 3

Psyrrí and Thissío

From Thissío metro, stroll to ancient Kerameikos, then stop at the Museum of Islamic Art in Psyrrí before lunch. For some contemporary art, head to the Benaki Annexe for a choice of temporary exhibitions (closed Mon–Wed). On Fri/Sat there's late opening so you can linger. Afterwards, a pleasant walk takes you to Petrálona or Thissío for dinner.

Day 4

Retail therapy

It's at weekends that you'll find the Monastiráki flea market in full swing. Continue north through the central bazaar to the picturesque Varvákio food hall; lunch is nearby at Diporto Agoras or Klimataria. Walk south to the Hephaisteion temple, the Stoa of Attalos and the ancient Agora, and then take in the Frissiras Museum in Pláka plus the nearby Temple of Olympian Zeus. After dinner, between May and September, enjoy a film at an outdoor cinema in Petrálona, Pláka or Thissío district.

OF **ATHENS**

Day 6

Peloponnese

The following morning, use the handy ferry from nearby Ágios Nikólaos to Égio on the Corinth Gulf's south coast. Take in ancient Corinth and Mycenae en route to Návplio, where you overnight.

Day 7

National Museum and Soúnio

If you're an early riser you might have time to return to Athens via ancient Epidauros, hand in the hire car and drop your bag off where you're staying, and take in the National Archaeological Museum with its seven millennia of treasures – all before a late lunch in Exárhia. Then take a bus from the Mavromatéon terminal down to Soúnio for its Poseidon temple; there are beaches with tavernas adjacent (as well as hotels).

Day 5

Delphi

Pick up a hire car and head west to ancient Delphi; you'll need to stay overnight in Aráhova, modern Delfí village or Galaxídi on the Corinth Gulf for a relaxed visit to both the sprawling site and the museum.

Day 8

Argo-Saronic Gulf

Take a hydrofoil or catamaran from Piraeus to the Argo-Saronic island of your choice. On Égina, savour lunch in the neoclassical capital, hiring a scooter to visit the Aphaea temple and medieval Paleohóra. On Ýdra, enjoy the car-free horseshoe-shaped harbour and perhaps a hike through the pines.

CONTENTS

📖 INTRODUCTION _____ 10

🏛 A BRIEF HISTORY _____ 14

🏛 WHERE TO GO _____ 29

The Acropolis _____ 29
The Propylaea and around 31, The Parthenon 34, The Erechtheion
and Porch of the Caryatids 36, Views from the Acropolis 37

Around the Acropolis _____ 38
The Odeion of Herodes Atticus (Iródio) 38, The Theatre
of Dionysos 39, New Acropolis Museum 39,
Filopappos Monument 40, The Pnyx and Areopagos hills 41,
Pláka and Anafiótika 43, Pláka museums 43, Cathedrals old
and new 45, The Roman Forum 46, The Greek Agora 47

Monastiráki _____ 52
Monastiráki Square 53, Benaki Museum of Islamic Art 54,
Herakleidon Museum 54, Kerameikos and Gázi 55

Omónia and environs _____ 57
The National Archaeological Museum 58

From Omónia to Sýndagma _____ 60
Neoclassical trilogy 61

Sýndagma Square and around _____ 62
Around Sýndagma 64, Vassilísis Sofías museums 66

Excursions **68**
Monastery of Kessarianí 68, Monastery of Dafní 68, Ancient
Eleusis 69, Brauron (Vravróna) 70, Soúnio 70, Piraeus 71, The
Saronic Gulf islands 72, The Argolid Peninsula 74, Delphi 80,
Ósios Loukás Monastery 81

😊 WHAT TO DO 83

Entertainment 83
Sports 85
Shopping 88
Children's Athens 92

😋 EATING OUT 94

🍴 A–Z TRAVEL TIPS 111

🛏 RECOMMENDED HOTELS 132

📖 INDEX 140

⊙ FEATURES

The ancient Greek pantheon 16
The law of *andiparohí* 25
Historical landmarks 27
A Greek who's who 32
Ottoman Athens 47
The Panathenaic Festival 51
Summer festivals 84
Calendar of events 93
Bulk wine and retsína 100

INTRODUCTION

Mention the name Athens, and almost everyone will have some preconceived ideas about the city. Socrates painted a verbal picture in the 4th century BC, Pausanias followed suit in the Roman era. Nineteenth-century travellers gave it an air of romance. During the 1960s, the Greek film industry added its own slant to the image with such movies as *Never on Sunday* and *The Red Lanterns*, and schoolchildren still learn about the 12 great gods of ancient Greece. Of late, it has become synonymous with periodic demonstrations and strikes, variably likely to impinge on a casual visit.

This small ancient city set on and around a dramatic hill of rock – the Acropolis – became the cradle of Western civilisation. During its 5th- and 4th-century BC heyday, Athenians were highly sophisticated in their thoughts and actions, their tastes and fashions. They left an enduring legacy of concepts and ideas for humankind, but also a remarkable number of buildings and artefacts that tell us about their lives. The remains of the buildings atop and around the Acropolis are instantly recognisable, and hundreds of statues, along with household pottery, jewellery and tools exert a fascination on anyone who enjoys exploring the past.

THE MODERN CAPITAL

The city of Athens is more than a sum of these ancient parts. After Constantinople became the capital of the eastern Roman Empire in 330 AD, Athens gradually shrank to little more than a village, only to rise phoenix-like from the ashes after 1834, the year it was designated capital of the modern Greek state. Neoclassical design was fashionable across Europe during the mid-19th century, and the impressive buildings then constructed in Athens could be

Bustling Monastiráki Square with the Acropolis in the background

seen beside their prototypes. In 1923, following the collapse of the Ottoman Empire and Greece's ultimately repelled invasion of Anatolia, Greece and republican Turkey agreed on a population exchange based on religious grounds which brought to Greece more than one million Orthodox Christians, resident in Asia Minor since antiquity. Athens strained to accommodate many of them in the first hastily erected suburbs around the central area. The result is that much of Athens is overbuilt, with congested, narrow streets and a shortage of green space and parking. The post-World War II policy of *andiparohí* also radically changed the look of the city (see page 25).

Today, the heart of Athens, the central, 19th-century triangular grid defined by Sýndagma (Sýntagma) and Omónia squares and the Kerameikos archaeological site, has been rejuvenated with pedestrianised streets, carefully renovated neoclassical buildings and attractive lighting. Just beyond, the

districts of Monastiráki and Pláka immediately south, and the Acropolis above these, contain many of the most interesting places to see.

ATHENIAN WAY OF LIFE

Athens is a city to be enjoyed outdoors. Every district has its own small, leafy squares with cafés and tavernas where people gather for a drink or meal. With kind prices, locals and visitors alike can enjoy delicious dishes that have been served for centuries, even in these straitened times.

The Athens and Epidaurus Festival, held annually in June and July, offers a full programme of music, dance and theatre at various outdoor venues. Both classical groups and name jazz artists perform at the indoor Mégaro Mousikís. League football and basketball, in which the Greeks have been enduringly successful, are also followed avidly.

Tradition still plays an important part in daily life. The family forms the backbone of Greek society and filial ties are strong. Children still play safely in the streets with *giagiá* (grandma) keeping a watchful eye; and new babies are proudly shown to the world during the evening *vólta* (stroll).

The Orthodox Church – long the symbolic unifier of the Greek diaspora, and constitutionally an established religion – has seen its influence wane considerably in recent decades. Religious observance remains strongest amongst older women, who still stop in the nearest church to reverence an icon or light a candle. But even the sceptical young will still be married in church, and have their offspring baptised there.

CRITICAL TIMES

Since joining the European Community in 1981, Greece has received huge sums in aid for upgrading infrastructure (especially transport and telecoms) throughout the country. However, it is now evident that Greece's accession to the euro in 2002 was helped along with doctored accounts, with an ensuing economic disaster. Greece has hovered on the brink of default in paying off a truly colossal debt to foreign banks since early 2010. In a 2015 referendum, the majority of Greeks voted not to accept a bailout tied to strict austerity measures, resulting in growing fears of a Greek exit from the EU (dubbed 'Grexit'). In 2016, a new compromise was reached: lenders agreed to restructure Greece's debts on the condition that Greece remained committed to a series of economic reforms. In February 2017, the Greek Finance Ministry announced government debt had reached €226.36 billion.

Amidst all of this, tourism remains Greece's major foreign currency earner, with more than 28 million visitors in a good year – over a third of these passing through Athens. Despite current woes, tourists find an open, lively and accessible city.

A BRIEF HISTORY

In ancient Greek mythology, Athens was named following a contest between Athena, goddess of wisdom, and Poseidon, god of the sea. Both coveted the city, so it was agreed that whoever produced the more useful gift for mortals would win.

First Poseidon struck the rock of the Acropolis with his mighty trident and brought salt water gushing forth. Then it was Athena's turn. She conjured an olive tree, which proved more useful and valuable. Thus she became the city's special protector.

ANCIENT CITY-STATE

The real story of the city-state of Athens is just as fascinating. The earliest Athenian settlement, dating from around 3000 BC, was built atop the Acropolis. During the late Bronze Age, also known as the Mycenaean era after King Agamemnon's famous Argolid city, a large palace was erected there too. For several centuries, the Mycenaeans dominated the eastern Mediterranean and Aegean. A long series of conflicts, however, including the legendary siege of Troy, weakened their militaristic civilisation.

The city-state of Athens came to occupy the entire Attic peninsula 50km (31 miles) south to Cape Sounion, northeast to the Rhamnous fortress, and southwest to Megara, a total of 3,885 sq km (1,500 sq miles). This extensive territory included some important natural resources. The broad Mesogeia plain was, and remains today, a productive farming area. The Laurio (today Lávrio) mines near Sounion yielded silver; the mountains of Ymittós and Pendéli provided marble for building; and both Pireás and Pórto Ráfti were large natural harbours – factors critical to Athenian strength.

TOWARDS DEMOCRACY

By the 6th century BC Athens was a major power. The first steps towards democracy were taken early in the 6th century BC under Solon, an Athenian merchant and poet appointed to reform the constitution. He cancelled all debts for which land or liberty could be forfeited and established a council *(boule)* of 400 members to formulate proposals discussed in the full assembly of adult male citizens.

The tyrant Peisistratos took power in the middle of the 6th century BC, and under his rule, commerce and the arts flourished. Attica's wine and olive oil were shipped to Italy, Egypt and Asia Minor; the first tragedies ever written were performed at the annual festival of Dionysos; and the standard version of Homer's works was set down.

Mosaic of Dionysos from a Roman villa, Corinth (2nd century AD)

⊙ THE ANCIENT GREEK PANTHEON

Following an Athens court ruling in May 2006, it is no longer illegal to worship the ancient Greek gods in Greece – and there are a surprising number of adherents of pagan ways (the *dodekathéistes*). Here's a summary of the main deities.

Zeus rules gods and mortals, and controls the weather; his symbols are the eagle, thunder and the oak tree. **Hera** is Zeus' third and oft-betrayed wife, patroness of marriage and motherhood. **Athena**, daughter of Zeus, is goddess of wisdom and crafts, guardian of war heroes, and supposed inventor of the loom and potter's wheel. **Apollo**, a son of Zeus, is the deity of music, healing, prophecy and the sun; his advice was sought at the Delphic oracle. **Artemis** is Apollo's twin sister, goddess of hunting and the moon, and guardian of animals and young virgins. **Hermes**, another son of Zeus, was the messenger of the gods, escort of dead souls and god of commerce, orators and writers, as well as protector of flocks, thieves and travellers. **Ares**, god of war, is yet another son of Zeus, but was unpopular on Olympos and understandably feared by mortals. Lame **Hephaestos**, god of fire and metallurgy, yet another sibling of Apollo and Ares, was the divine blacksmith, furnishing Zeus with his thunderbolts. He was married to (and frequently cuckolded by) **Aphrodite**, goddess of love, beauty and gardens. **Poseidon**, brother of Zeus, presided over seas, rivers and all creatures therein, causing storms and earthquakes with his trident; horses were also sacred to him. **Hades**, another brother of Zeus, ruled the kingdom of the dead – but also controlled all mineral wealth beneath the earth. **Demeter**, sister of Zeus, is the goddess of agriculture and protectress of crops, having bestowed corn, grain and the plough on mankind.

Further constitutional and electoral reforms were made in 508 BC under Kleisthenes who created 10 artificial tribes, each based on domicile rather than blood-ties and consisting of the same number of people from the city, coast and inland. These provided military support, elected officials, and sent representatives to a new council of 500 members, which replaced Solon's 400-member council. However, all this co-existed with extensive recourse to slavery, with captives brought from Thrace and Asia Minor to work the Laurio mines in particular.

PERSIAN WARS

In the 5th century BC, the Athenians stopped the great Persian Empire from invading from the east: in 490 BC, their army defeated a Persian force sent by Darius I on the plain of Marathon, just 43km (26 miles) northeast of Athens. According to legend, the soldier who ran from Marathon to Athens died of exhaustion immediately after reporting the victory. His feat is commemorated in the 26-mile Olympic marathon.

Ten years later Darius I's son, Xerxes, occupied Athens and burned the Acropolis, only to see his own fleet destroyed by the Athenian navy.

PELOPONNESIAN WAR, MACEDONIAN RULE

Following the Persian Wars, Athens and Sparta were the two most powerful Greek city-states. Each sought dominance, until their rivalry erupted in the long Peloponnesian War (431–404 BC), which ended in Athenian defeat. The repressive government installed by the Spartans in Athens was soon overthrown, and the Athenians joined Persia to defeat the Spartan navy in 394 BC. In 338 BC Athens and Thebes, now allied against the common threat of Macedonia under Philip II, were defeated in Boeotia. Philip became the ruler of mainland Greece until his assassination, when he was succeeded by his son Alexander (later the Great). Their rule of Athens was benign, and despite strong resentment of Macedonian rule, the city flourished.

CLASSICAL, HELLENISTIC AND ROMAN PERIODS

The 157 years between the victory over the Persians at Salamis in 480 BC and the death of Alexander the Great in 323 BC were years of extraordinary intellectual and cultural activity for Athens.

The great philosophers Socrates, Plato and Aristotle lived during this period, as did the playwrights Aristophanes and Sophocles, the historians Herodotos and Thucydides, the sculptors Phidias and Praxiteles, and the statesman Pericles. The work of these and many other gifted men laid the groundwork for much of European civilisation. Many of the physical remains of this extraordinary flowering are concentrated on the Acropolis and in the centre of the ancient city, the Greek Agora.

The Romans patronised Athens after taking control of Greece in 146 BC, coming to the city to study. Julius Caesar had the Roman Agora built just east of the Athenian Agora, and Hadrian (emperor AD 117–138) commissioned the construction of the Library of Hadrian while completing the Olympian Zeus temple. In the 3rd century AD the Heruli, a Germanic tribe expelled from Scandinavia by the Danes, appeared in the Black Sea and continued south to wreak havoc in Greece. They burned Athens in AD 267 before moving on to sack Corinth, Sparta and Argos.

BYZANTINE EMPIRE

When the Roman emperor Constantine designated Byzantium (ie Constantinople – present-day İstanbul) as his new capital in AD 330, the Empire became divided into eastern and western

Carved flower detail, ancient Greek Agora

MAXIMIA

Mosaic in the Byzantine Museum

sectors. Rome was soon to fall to successive waves of invaders, while Constantinople thrived. Athens continued to serve as a great cultural and educational centre until 529, when the Christian emperor Justinian I ordered that all pagan philosophical schools in Athens be closed. The Parthenon and other temples elsewhere had already been turned into churches in 435. But the demise of the schools led to the city's decline into an unimportant provincial town.

In 1204 the Fourth Crusade sacked Orthodox Christian Byzantium, and Athens was constituted under a Latin Catholic duchy under Burgundian, Catalan and Florentine overlords.

OTTOMAN OCCUPATION

Byzantium fell in 1453 to Mehmet II and the Ottoman Turks, who reached Athens three years later. Many Albanian Christians, who had served as mercenary troops for both the

Byzantines and the Ottomans, moved to Athens and settled in Pláka.

The Turks made the Acropolis a Muslim precinct and the city acquired three purpose-built mosques, as well as three hamams (bath-houses). The Ottomans also transformed a number of churches into mosques, including the Parthenon on the Acropolis, which acquired a minaret.

The Ottoman occupation of Athens was interrupted by war with the Venetians in 1687. Besieged on the Acropolis that September, the Turks were using the Parthenon for storing munitions. The Venetian commander, Count Morosini, brought his artillery, manned by Swedish mercenaries, to the nearby Filopáppos hill. One shell scored a direct hit on the powder magazine, and the resulting explosion was devastating. Many Turks were killed, the Acropolis village was set alight and the Parthenon suffered major damage for the first time.

The Turks surrendered and departed, the Venetians controlling the city until lack of men and a severe outbreak of plague forced them to leave by April 1688. The Athenians, who had welcomed the Christian Venetians but feared retribution after the inevitable Ottoman return, also fled Athens, leaving it uninhabited for three years. During the second period of Ottoman occupation, Pláka became the city's central commercial area.

Athenian houses at this time were normally built with a courtyard and, for both privacy and protection, they had few or no windows opening onto the narrow, haphazard streets. Most were two storeys high with the kitchen and storerooms on the ground floor; a wooden verandah, bedrooms, and the family common room were on the upper floor. Usually there were two knockers on the front door: one for servants and peasants; and another fancier one higher up for members of the family and upper-class visitors.

FIGHT FOR INDEPENDENCE

The Greek War of Independence began in the Peloponnese in 1821, and the Athenians expelled the Turks from Athens the following June, with much attendant massacre. Ottoman forces returned in 1826 to besiege the city, capturing the Acropolis in June 1827. The Greeks were obliged to sign a treaty turning Athens over to the Turks, after which the Athenians retired to the Argo-Saronic islands. The real issue was decided a few months later when, on 20 October 1827, a combined British, French and Russian fleet defeated the Turco-Egyptian fleet at Navarino on the west coast of the Peloponnese.

In 1830 the London Protocol was signed by Britain, France, Russia and Turkey recognising Greece as an independent kingdom. Otto of Bavaria was made King of Greece in 1832, and the last Turkish troops on the Acropolis surrendered in March 1833. In October 1834 Athens was officially declared the capital of Greece.

At the time, the city was little more than a village, with a population of about 4,000. During ancient times, the population had reached 36,000. Several grandiose plans were submitted, including one to build a large palace on the Acropolis. Instead Sýndagma (Constitution) Square was chosen as the site for the royal palace, now the Parliament building. The overall city plan was based on wide boulevards and squares within a triangle of three main streets, today Ermoú, Pireós and Stadíou. Ermoú runs from Sýndagma Square to the Kerameikos archaeological site; Pireós runs from Omónia Square past Kerameikos to the port of Piraeus; and Stadíou runs from Omónia Square to Sýndagma Square. This triangle still defines the heart of old Athens.

Strong German influence upon the designs of the buildings erected in post-independence Athens meant that the revival of Classical architecture in Greece was not based directly on examples of Classical antiquity, but on the neoclassical style popular

Neoclassical facade of the Academy, built between 1859–87

in western Europe. The University of Athens on Panepistemíou Street is a fine example of this imported paradigm.

In 1862 King Otto was deposed and replaced by a young prince from the Danish house of Glücksberg, who became George I, reigning successfully until 1913.

EARLY 20TH CENTURY

Within just three years of becoming Greece's capital, the population of Athens had increased almost fourfold, and steady growth continued thereafter. A particularly large wave of immigration occurred in 1922–3, the result of a significant exchange of populations: approximately 390,000 Muslims left Greece for Turkey and almost 1,500,000 Greeks moved from western Anatolia and eastern Thrace to Greece.

Between 1936 and 1941 Greece was under the military dictatorship of Ioannis Metaxas, who rejected Mussolini's demand

that Greece give safe passage to the Italian army. During the winter of 1940–41 the Greek army stopped the Italian advance into Greek Epirus, a heroic accomplishment commemorated each year with a national holiday on 28 October.

In April 1941, Germany invaded Greece, defeating all Allied forces there by early June with the country divided into Bulgarian, German and Italian occupation zones. Many Athenians starved during the following winter as all food was requisitioned. The Greek resistance movement, well established by mid-1942, became so politically divided that guerrilla fighters expended almost as much energy fighting each other as they did fighting the Axis. In October 1944, Allied forces moved into Athens, encountering no opposition from the retreating Germans.

The war left Greece utterly devastated. Communist and royalist partisans moved steadily towards a military confrontation as the United States, under the Truman Doctrine, supported the central government. Three years of savage civil war ended in late 1949 with communist defeat. Political instability and repression persisted through the 1950s and early 1960s.

REIGN OF THE JUNTA

On 21 April 1967, the military seized power and tanks rolled on to the streets of Athens. During the seven-year dictatorship of the junta, initially under Colonel George Papadopoulos (most of the junta were actually generals), political parties were dissolved, the press was censored and left-wing sympathisers were exiled or tortured and imprisoned. In December 1967, King Constantine II led an ineffective counter-coup and was obliged to leave the country. In June 1973 Greece was declared a republic, with Papadopoulos as its first president. On 17 November of the same year a major student protest at Athens Polytechnic was brutally crushed by armoured vehicles, leaving dozens killed. The end came eight months later when the junta overthrew the Cypriot president, Archbishop Makarios, provoking the Turkish invasion

---

⊘ THE LAW OF *ANDIPAROHÍ*

The 1950s policy of *andiparohí* drastically changed the appearance of a city that had grown organically since the 1830s. Under this law, the owners of a shack or crumbling mansion alike could hand their property to a developer, who would knock it down and erect a block of flats, with two or three flats allotted to the provider of the site in exchange. Both parties benefited: the developer didn't have to buy land, and the donating family received free real estate. But Athens suffered aesthetically as dreary concrete apartments spread everywhere up till the 1970s.

of Cyprus. The junta's subsequent order to move against Turkey was so suicidal that senior military commanders in turn overthrew the junta. Constantine Karamanlís, the former conservative premier, was recalled from exile in Paris to restore democracy. The reforms that followed included a referendum that definitively abolished the monarchy.

THE WAY FORWARD

In 1981, the year that it entered the EC, Greece elected its first nominally socialist government under charismatic Andreas Papandreou and his PASOK party. Papandreou, while excluding the recently legalised Communist Party from government, finally recognised the communist and leftist resistance organisations who had fought against the Axis World War II occupation. This was a major contribution to political stability, as was the 1989 destruction of all secret-police files. PASOK held power for most of the next three decades, before their support plummeted drastically as a result of the financial crisis and their acceptance of unpopular austerity measures – PASOK's George Papandreou resigned as prime minister in November 2011.

In January 2015, the SYRIZA party celebrated their first ever victory in Greece's parliamentary elections. With Alexis Tsipras as prime minister, SYRIZA formed a coalition government with the Independent Greeks party (ANEL); just months later, disagreements over the financial crisis saw Tsipras resign, only to be reinstated in September 2015. While Greece's economic troubles continue – exacerbated by the refugee crisis – in mid-2016 a new deal was struck with the troika (comprising the IMF, the European Commission and the European Central Bank) under which the lenders agreed to restructure Greece's debt programme dependent upon Greece implementing a range of radical reforms.

HISTORICAL LANDMARKS

1150–750 BC Post-Mycenaean Dark Age.

750–480 BC The Archaic Period.

594–93 BC Solon breaks aristocratic power.

508 BC Kleisthenes introduces limited democracy in Athens.

490 BC First Persian War: Greeks win at Marathon.

480 BC Athenian fleet defeats Persians in the Strait of Salamis.

477 BC Athens unites allies under the Delian League.

459–429 BC The Golden Age of Pericles.

431–404 BC Peloponnesian War; Sparta defeats Athens.

338 BC Philip II of Macedon acquires Athens.

336–323 BC Alexander the Great rules Greece.

323–146 BC The Hellenistic Period.

146 BC–AD 330 Roman rule.

AD 49–50 St Paul brings Christianity to Athens.

529 Byzantine emperor Justinian orders closure of all philosophy schools.

1204 Latin Crusaders take Athens.

1456 Athens falls to the Ottoman Turks.

1687 Venetians besiege Athens; Parthenon blown up.

1821–33 Greek War of Independence.

1834 Athens becomes the capital of Greece.

1923 Greeks from Asia Minor flood into Athens.

1941–4 Axis powers occupy Greece.

1946–9 Greek Civil War ends with Communist defeat.

1951 Greece becomes a member of NATO.

1967–74 Military junta rules Greece.

1981 Greece joins the EC.

2002 The euro replaces the drachma.

2004 Athens hosts Olympic Games.

2010–11 Greek debt burden becomes unmanageable.

2015 Alexis Tsipras (SYRIZA) becomes prime minister.

2015–16 Refugee numbers swell. Greece negotiates bailout deal.

2017 Government debt reaches €226.36 billion.

Athens and the Acropolis lit up at night

WHERE TO GO

Viewed from the air – or from the heights of the Acropolis or Mount Lykavitós – Athens is a sprawling maze of apartment blocks and office buildings stretching to the horizon. Yet central Athens is remarkably compact. Most major sites are within walking distance of one another, while the metro and bus systems provide inexpensive, reliable transport for those who become footsore.

Ancient remains and worthwhile museums are scattered across the central area. Athens has grown incrementally over time, resulting in numerous districts, each with its own particular character. This guide divides the city into a number of sections, covering the ancient centre first and then moving out in a clockwise spiral through the other important neighbourhoods.

Ancient Athens was focused on the Acropolis, with sacred temples built atop the rock and the town spread out below. Today the area is still replete with Greek and Roman remains, albeit interspersed with later buildings – a fascinating mixture of neoclassical mansions and terraced cottages dating back to Ottoman times. This area, Pláka, is one of the most charming parts of Athens.

THE ACROPOLIS

It's impossible to overestimate the importance of the **Acropolis** ❶ (daily Apr–Oct 8am–6.30pm, Nov–Mar until 5pm) to the ancient Greeks. The religious significance of this sheer-sided rock, looming 90m (300ft) above Athens, was paramount, and the buildings on the summit still embody the essence of classical Greek architecture. You can see these temples from most parts of the city – particularly at night when they are beautifully

Exploring the Acropolis

lit – which adds to the feeling that this small area is still the heart of Athens. The name 'Acropolis' derives from the Greek words *ákro*, meaning 'highest point', and *pólis*, meaning town.

Try to visit early or late in the day to avoid the tour groups, or on Mondays, when most tours don't operate; wear comfortable rubber-soled shoes as there are slippery stones worn smooth over the centuries and numerous uneven areas where heels can catch.

Once past the ticket office, a path leads to the summit of the Acropolis – a relatively flat plateau around 320m by 130m (1,050ft by 425ft) in area. This steep incline is the last section of the original route taken by the Panathenaic procession up to the statue of Athena (see page 51).

Used for strategic purposes throughout the Mycenaean and Archaic periods, the rock was easy to defend. It had spring water and superb views of the surrounding area. The first religious structures appeared at the end of the 6th century BC, though these early temples were destroyed by the Persians under Xerxes in 480 BC. The Athenians left the gutted temples untouched for three decades and were only persuaded by Pericles to undertake a reconstruction programme in 449 BC.

Pericles commissioned the Parthenon, the Erechtheion, the Temple of Athena Nike and the Propylaea, taking advantage of a new marble quarry on Mount Pendéli (Pentele to the ancients); the marble thus became known as Pentelic. When the Romans took control of Athens they embellished the site with small additions, but the decline of Roman power left the Acropolis vulnerable to attack and vandalism. The rock reverted to its earliest use as a strategic stronghold during Ottoman rule. Large quantities of stone from the temples were used for construction of bastions and domestic buildings.

Following Greek independence in the 19th century, a zealous restoration project saw the removal of all medieval and Ottoman structures on the Acropolis, and inaugurated archaeological studies of the ancient remains. These continue to the present day.

THE PROPYLAEA AND AROUND

As you make your way up towards the Propylaea (gateway) you will pass through the **Beule Gate Ⓐ**, built as part of a 3rd-century AD defensive wall. This gate was revealed only in 1853, underneath an Ottoman bastion. Immediately past this stands the jewelbox-like **Athena Nike temple Ⓑ**, among the earliest Periclean projects, with four Ionic columns at the front and rear; since the millennium it has been completely reconstructed, using original masonry chunks. In myth, King Aegeus leapt to his death from here upon spying the ship of his son Theseus, who had neglected to change his sails from black to white as a sign of having successfully vanquished the Cretan Minotaur.

More like a temple than a gateway, the monumental **Propylaea** was a sign of things to come, built to impress visitors. It retains this ability in modern times, even though

⊙ A GREEK WHO'S WHO

As the cradle of democracy, history, philosophy, drama and comedy, it's not surprising that Athens was the birthplace of some of the most illustrious figures in ancient history. Here are just a few:

Socrates (c. 469–399 BC): philosopher and orator who pursued truth through dialectic discourse.

Plato (c. 428–347 BC): student of Socrates, political and religious philosopher; founded his own academy of higher study.

Aristotle (384–322 BC): philosopher; student at Plato's academy and tutor to Alexander the Great.

Herodotos (484–425 BC): 'Father of history'; wrote thorough accounts of the early Persian wars and dynastic struggles in Asia Minor.

Thucydides (c. 460–400 BC): chronicled the Peloponnesian Wars with the first analytical methodology for recording history.

Pericles (c. 495–429 BC): Athenian statesman during the city's Golden Age; responsible for construction of the Parthenon.

Kallikrates and **Iktinos**: architects of the Parthenon (447–432 BC).

Pheidias (c. 490–430 BC) and **Praxiteles**: sculptors.

Aiskhylos (525–456 BC), **Sophokles** (497–406 BC) and **Euripides** (480–406 BC): great tragic dramatists; Euripides in particular wrote plays about ordinary mortals rather than mortals interacting with gods.

Aristophanes (448–385 BC): originator of Greek comedy.

The Propylaea seen from below

the structure was never actually completed. Construction commenced in 437 BC to a plan by the brilliant Athenian architect Mnesikles. A series of six Doric columns marks the transition into the Propylaea, beyond which there are four symmetrical rooms, two on either side of the walkway. Two rows of three Ionic columns (this was the first building to incorporate both styles of column) support the roof, whose coffered ceiling was originally painted as a heavenly scene. The five heavy wooden doors along the walkway would have heightened the anticipation of ancient pilgrims, as each would be opened in turn. The only room to have been completed was the second on the northern side. This was used as a refuge for visitors to the Acropolis and also, according to the 2nd-century AD travelling geographer Pausanias, as a picture gallery *(Pinakotheke)*, since its walls were covered with panels and frescoes.

Just beyond the Propylaea, you will find on your right remains of the **Sanctuary of Artemis Brauronia ⓓ**, founded in the 4th century BC.

THE PARTHENON

The **Parthenon ⓔ** is one of the most recognisable buildings in the world. The series of columns supporting pediment and frieze is the epitome of Athens to many visitors, and would also have been to travellers in ancient times. However, they would have seen a highly coloured structure decorated with magnificently carved sculptures, not to mention a strong wooden roof. What remains is the bare Pentelic marble used in the construction, and the refined lines and form that make it an architectural masterpiece.

The Parthenon was dedicated to Athena, goddess of wisdom and justice, and means Temple of the Virgin. It also housed the city's treasury, thus combining spiritual and secular wealth. An Archaic temple on the site was removed after the battle of Marathon in 490 BC to make room for a much larger temple. This so-called older Parthenon was still being constructed when the Persians destroyed the Acropolis temples in 480 BC. Work on the present temple, designed by Kallikrates and Iktinos, began in 447 BC. The temple was dedicated to Athena in 438 BC, at the

Optical illusion

There are no straight lines anywhere in the Parthenon; the ancient designers deliberately used a technique known as *entasis*, with gradual curves in lintels, stairways or pediments, and columns with bulging centres. This sophisticated optical illusion leaves the impression that the building is in fact completely squared on the vertical and horizontal.

Panathenaic Festival. This festival then took place every four years until the late 4th century AD (see page 51).

The Parthenon was converted into a church in the 6th century, and a bell tower was added by the Byzantines who named it Agía Sofía, meaning the Holy Wisdom. During the 15th century, under Ottoman rule, the bell tower became a minaret and the church was converted into a mosque.

Eventually the building served as a munitions store. In September 1687, when Venetian forces attacked Athens, a shell hit the Parthenon, igniting the powder inside. The resulting explosion destroyed the centre of the temple along with many priceless carved friezes and columns. Under a 'licence' from the sultan, Lord Elgin removed as much of the Parthenon's sculpture as his men could cut free, a process that continued from 1801 until 1811. The items, known as the **Elgin Marbles**, are on display in the British Museum, though the legitimacy of retaining them is hotly

The Porch of the Caryatids

disputed. Restoration on what remains of the temple has been almost constant since 1834.

Today it is not possible to walk among the columns and the temple interior. This echoes the rules of ancient Greece, when only the highest priests could enter the *naos* or central sanctuary. There they would have worshipped an ivory-and-gold-covered wooden statue of Athena said to have been 12m (39ft) high. Walk around the 70m-by-30m (230ft-by-100ft) exterior to appreciate the colonnades.

THE ERECHTHEION AND PORCH OF THE CARYATIDS

To the north of the Parthenon stand the graceful statues of the **Porch of the Caryatids**, which adorn the southern facade of the **Erechtheion** ⑤. This temple is an unusual mélange of styles, with rooms at varying levels, built on the putative site of Athena and Poseidon's contest for the honour of protecting Athens. It was the last of Pericles' great buildings to be finished, dedicated in 406 BC, and combined the worship of Athena and Poseidon under one roof. Following the contest between the two gods, legend has it that they were reconciled and this dual temple recognised their special bond with the city. The sanctuary was converted into a church in the 6th century AD and was used to house the governor's harem during Ottoman times.

The **caryatids** – female figures used as pillars – are so named because they were long presumed to be depictions of the women from Peloponnesian Karyai, captured after that city-state made an alliance with the Persians and was sacked in punishment. Now, however, it is thought more likely that they represent local novices in the service of the goddess Athena. The on-site sculptures are copies: five of the originals are displayed in the New Acropolis Museum; the sixth, taken by Elgin, is in the British Museum. On the eastern facade a row of Ionic columns marks the entrance to the sanctuary of Athena Polias, established here after the original Temple of Athena was destroyed by the Persians in 480 BC. The foundations of this **Old Temple of Athena** are in a roped-off area directly south of the Erechtheion.

The Erechtheion's north facade consists of another porch, on high foundations since the ground level drops here. A hole in the ceiling and a gap in the floor were left to show where Poseidon had struck with his trident. The name Erechtheion derives from Erechtheos, legendary Archaic king of Athens and predecessor of Kekrops, whose tomb was supposedly beneath the building. Outside the porch to the west was located a now-vanished altar to Zeus, said to be beneath the olive tree Athena gave to the city.

VIEWS FROM THE ACROPOLIS

When you've finished exploring the Acropolis, take time to enjoy the views from its walls, some of which date back to the Mycenaean era. From the northeast corner, by the flag pole, you can see several of the other major archaeological sites and the district of Pláka below. The wooded slopes of Mount Lykavitós, with the smart area of Kolonáki on its lower slopes, is to the northeast. The coast and the islands of the Saronic Gulf lie to the southwest.

AROUND THE ACROPOLIS

A number of other archaeological remains – including the Odeion of Herodes Atticus, the Theatre of Dionysos, the Monument of Philopappos, the Hill of the Pnyx and the Hill of Areopagos – can be found on the flanks of the Acropolis and on nearby hills. Head south of the rock by turning left out of the main entrance and you will reach the first after a five-minute walk.

THE ODEION OF HERODES ATTICUS (IRÓDIO)

The **Odeion of Herodes Atticus G** (the Iródio in modern Greek) was built in AD 161–174 in Roman style with a three-storey stage and an auditorium capable of seating 5,000 spectators. It was destroyed during the 3rd century AD, while in the 18th

The Odeion of Herodes Atticus

century the Ottomans used material from the ruins to build a defensive wall. In the 1950s it was restored and now provides the venue for spectacular outdoor summer performances held during the **Athens and Epidauros Festival** (see page 84).

THE THEATRE OF DIONYSOS

Set into the hillside on the southeastern flank of the Acropolis are the extensive remains of the **Theatre of Dionysos** ⓗ (daily May–Oct 8am–6.30pm, Nov–Apr until 5pm), built in the 5th century BC and upgraded two centuries later. In Roman times, the Stoa of Eumenes, of which little remains, linked it with the Odeion of Herodes Atticus. The theatre, capacity 17,000, was the birthplace of dramatic and comic art and formed the social and political heart of Athens during its 'golden age'. The premieres of several major pieces by Sophokles, Euripides and Aristophanes were performed here, and the Athenian assembly also met here late in its history. Most interesting are the carved front-row thrones for VIPs, including one with lion's-claw feet reserved for the high priest of Dionysos. The so-called **Stage of Phaedros** depicting scenes from the life of Dionysos dates from the 4th century BC.

NEW ACROPOLIS MUSEUM

Opposite the Dionysos theatre stands the shining modern construction of the **New Acropolis Museum** ❷ (Apr–Oct Mon 8am–4pm, Tue–Thu and Sat–Sun until 8pm, Fri until 10pm, Nov–Mar Mon–Thu 9am–5pm, Fri until 10pm, Sat–Sun until 8pm; www.theacropolismuseum.gr), inaugurated after many delays in 2009 at a cost of €130 million.

The stark, angular structure seems distinctly retrograde from outside, but the interior with its clever natural lighting does an admirable job of showcasing the contents, many never before exhibited owing to the space limitations of the old museum.

The lowest gallery houses finds from the Acropolis slopes. Leading to the upper levels is a ramp, simulating the approach to the Acropolis, surveyed by the scarred but still impressive, original Caryatids (which have recently undergone three-and-a-half years of laser cleaning). On the first floor, the Archaic exhibition features the famous Moskhophoros (Calf-Bearer), and various coquettish *korai* revealing a pre-Classical ideal of beauty in their make-up, earrings and crinkled, close-fitting garments. The top floor is the pièce de résistance: a glass gallery holding a reconstruction of the **Parthenon pediments**, of the same size and compass orientation as the actual Parthenon looming just outside the wrap-around windows. The friezes, including the triangular western aetoma, are mounted at eye level – unlike their original position overshadowed by eaves so that the ancient Athenians couldn't really appreciate them. Authentic fragments which Greece retains – less than half the total – have been mounted alongside plaster casts of the originals in the British Museum, a pointed exercise in advocacy for their return.

During construction (2004–07), parts of ancient Athens were discovered on site. This was one reason for the delay in the opening: building plans were altered so that dwellings, wells, water and sewage works, an olive press and even a symposium hall with mosaic flooring remained viewable through glass panels set in the ground. The excavations extend well under the museum, suspended above them by 100 massive anti-seismic columns.

FILOPAPPOS MONUMENT

Southwest of the Acropolis stands the **Monument of Filopappos ❸**, built in AD 116 for the last titular ruler of Commagene. This small Hellenic kingdom located in southeastern Anatolia was independent from 162 BC until AD 72. When Philopappos lived in Athens as a Roman consul there was no longer a Commagene to rule but he was generous to his adopted city, which responded with this impressive funeral monument. The convex facade has a sculptured frieze depicting Philopappos riding a chariot and performing his duties in the senate. The view of the Acropolis from atop Filopáppos hill, as it is now called, is incomparable; the easiest way up is by paved path from the brilliantly frescoed Byzantine church of **Ágios Dimítrios Lombardiáris**  of the 15th century, a popular venue for weddings and baptisms.

The Monument of Filopappos

THE PNYX AND AREOPAGOS HILLS

North of Ágios Dimítrios Lombardiáris rises the **Hill of the Pnyx** ❺, meeting place of the Assembly of Athens. Loosely translated, pnyx means 'crowded or tightly packed place', and in ancient times this was a highly populated area. You'll see the outlines of walls, including the defensive **Themistoklean Wall**, between nearby shrubbery. The Pnyx meeting place can be found below the summit on the northeastern side of the hill. When democracy was established at the end of the 6th century BC, the debating chamber moved from the Agora to this

The Athens Observatory, on the Hill of the Pnyx

structure, where prominent public figures made their speeches at the rostrum. Seats were provided for the 5,000 citizens of the city needed for a decision-making quorum, who would listen to the arguments of the likes of Pericles and Themistokles. On the **Hill of the Nymphs** north of the Pnyx you'll see the neoclassical Athens Observatory, founded in 1842.

On the north flank of the Acropolis is the **Areopagos Hill ❻**, diagonally down to the north of the main Acropolis ticket office. This was the meeting place for the governing council in aristocratic periods, and remained the court of criminal justice even in the democratic era; the modern Greek supreme court is still called the *Áreos Págos* (Hill of Mars). Here in AD 51 St Paul delivered his speech known as the *Sermon on the Unknown God*, making an important convert in the judge Dionysios, henceforth the Areopagite and later second bishop of Athens (the nearby, pedestrianised street commemorates him). A bronze plaque with the sermon in Greek is to the right of the slippery steps leading to the top.

PLÁKA AND ANAFIÓTIKA

After exploring these fascinating sites, you should make your way towards the modern city via two small districts offering a range of cafés and tavernas, along with images of domestic life not found in more modern parts of Athens.

Anafiótika ❼ hugs the high ground immediately below the Acropolis, and can be reached semi-directly from the Areopagos. Built during the 19th century by skilled construction workers from the small Cycladic island of Anáfi, today the narrow lanes with their neat, whitewashed cottages – less than 50 remain – and potted geraniums are still reminiscent of their Aegean roots.

Pláka ❽ lies below Anafiótika and fills the space between the ancient and modern city, extending almost to Mitropóleos and Filellínon streets. This was the centre of population from Byzantine times through to Greek independence. The maze of narrow, occasionally pedestrianised thoroughfares with many neoclassical mansions and humbler houses is a delight to explore.

Pláka is particularly atmospheric in the evenings when visitors stroll before dinner and tavernas set tables out on the narrower lanes; these open out onto quiet squares often dominated by Byzantine churches or older monuments. The neoclassical buildings are now strictly protected, and this is the one part of the city which, superficially at least, gives a taste of what Athens before 1900 was like.

PLÁKA MUSEUMS

At Monís Asteríou 37, housed in a sumptuous neoclassical mansion, the **Frissiras Museum ❾** (Wed–Fri 10am–5pm, Sat–Sun 11am–5pm; www.frissirasmuseum.com) is among Athens'

Contemporary art on display at the Frissiras Museum

recent wave of small, excellent art museums based on private collections; it specialises in contemporary European painting and worthwhile temporary exhibits from the edgier side of the spectrum. Nearby at Níkis 39, the **Jewish Museum of Greece** ❿ (Mon–Fri 9am–2.30pm, Sun–10am–2pm; www.jewishmuseum. gr) tells the story of the various Jewish communities across the country, including the sad events of the 1940s when most Greek Jewry was wiped out.

At the southern end of Adrianoú, in a small square surrounded by cafés, stands the **Monument to Lysikratos** ⓫. Dating from the 4th century BC, its series of curved panels and columns create a circular structure supporting a dome made from a single block of Pentelic marble. Originally, this was topped by a bronze tripod – a prize awarded in choral competitions during the Classical era. During the 18th century a Capuchin monastery occupied the land all around the monument and the interior of the base was used as a guest room. Lord Byron stayed in 1810, supposedly penning part of *Childe Harold* here.

High up near the Acropolis, the **Kanellopoulos Museum** ⓬ (Tue–Sun 8am–3pm; www.pacanellopoulosfoundation.org) occupies a mansion at Pánou 12. This eclectic family collection, some found in a stylish new wing, encompasses Geometric-to-Hellenistic-period artwork, Roman funerary ornaments from Fayum, and Byzantine icons, jewellery, frescoes and tapestries. A few doors down at no. 22 is an engaging annexe of the Greek Folk Art Museum, **Man and Tools** (Wed–Mon 8am–3pm; www. melt.gr), full of pre-industrial processes and implements.

CATHEDRALS OLD AND NEW

From the Kanellopoulos and Man and Tools museums, walk straight down Mnisikléous to the vicinity of Athens' two cathedrals. Ground was broken for the rather gaudy new **Mitrópolis** ⓭ in 1842; it was completed in 1862, financed by the sale of land and structures pertaining to 72 other churches.

The cathedral houses the relics of Agía Filothéi, martyred by the Ottomans in 1589. She appeared in a vision to the faithful in 1940, foretelling Greece's ordeal during the occupation but victorious emergence thereafter. To the left of the entrance is also the marble sarcophagus of Patriarch Grigorios (Gregory) V, executed by the Ottomans in Istanbul when the Greek war of independence erupted in 1821, and whose corpse (after numerous adventures) only arrived here in 1871.

In the shadow of the main cathedral huddles the tiny **Mikrí Mitrópolis** (Little Cathedral), doubly dedicated to the Panagía Gorgoepikoös (She Who is Quick to Hear) and Ágios Elefthérios, protector of women in childbirth. Dating from the 12th century, the church was built using stone from various ancient structures. Wander around its exterior walls to

Mikrí Mitrópolis

see sections of Greek and Roman columns, or fragments of ornate carvings.

THE ROMAN FORUM

Where Adrianoú intersects Eólou, turn south on the latter to reach the **Roman Forum** ⑭ (daily 8am–5pm), first established during the 2nd century BC to accommodate an expanding Athens.

The ornate entrance gate was commissioned by Julius Caesar in honour of Athena in her avatar of Archegetis (Commander of the City). Much of the north and west wall of the Agora lies unexcavated under the houses of Pláka, but the south wall and the remains of the south colonnade are there, along with a series of shops. The most remarkable building in the complex (though it was outside the Agora when built) is the **Tower of the Winds**. This octagonal structure was a *klepsydra* or water-clock built by a Syrian Greek, Andronikos Kyrristos, in the 1st century BC. Each of the eight faces is decorated with a beautiful relief depicting a personification of the wind blowing from that direction. The timing device was driven by water piped down from the Acropolis.

Just west of the Tower of the Winds you'll see one of only two mosques still standing in Athens, the **Fethiye Tzami**. Built shortly after the Ottoman conquest, it now serves as an archaeological storehouse and is not open to the public.

THE GREEK AGORA

From the south side of the Roman Forum, continue west along Polygnótou to the southeast entrance of the ancient **Greek Agora** ⓯ (daily 8am–3pm), birthplace of western democracy and the social, commercial and administrative heart of the ancient city-state of Athens (*agora* is derived from the Greek *agiero*, meaning to assemble). From the 6th century BC onwards, this area played host to a number of activities including religious and political

⊙ OTTOMAN ATHENS

Until recently locals have not been keen to highlight monuments erected by the Ottoman conquerors, but it was the juxtaposition of the elements of an oriental bazaar with remains of the more distant past that most intrigued the first Grand Tourists who showed up in Athens late in the 18th century. The Ottomans did not consider Athens an especially important town, endowing it with just three purpose-built mosques (not counting churches converted for Islamic worship). These were the Fethiye and Tzidarakis mosques, and the Küçuk Tzami, just south of the Roman agora, though only foundations of the latter remain. There were also several *hamams* (bath-houses), though the only survivor is the intriguing Abdi Efendi baths at Kirrýstou 8 (Wed–Mon 8am–3pm; www.melt. gr), built in phases from the 15th to the 17th centuries. Nearby, opposite the Tower of the Winds, stands the surviving gateway of a 1721-vintage *medresse* or Koranic academy, later used as a prison and demolished around 1900. The Tower of the Winds itself (*Aérides* in modern Greek) served during the Ottoman period as a lodge of a dervish order, who terrified their Orthodox neighbours with their chanting and dancing.

meetings, law courts, education, shopping or simply passing the time. Here Socrates presented his philosophical theories; unfortunately he fell foul of the authorities and was put to death in 403 BC. The area was mostly razed during the Goth attacks of AD 267, but was covered with new buildings during Byzantine and Ottoman times, all of which had to be cleared when excavations began.

From the southeastern entrance, follow a section of the Panathenaic Way past the 11th-century church of **Ágii Apóstoli**, the only remaining Byzantine building on the site. Greatly changed over the centuries, it was restored to its original form in the late 1950s. The frescoes in the narthex are original; others were moved from the Hephaisteion when it was deconsecrated. The Panathenaic Way continues to the other entrance off Adrianoú, near which lies the **Altar of the Twelve Gods**. This small monument, from where distances to all other points in the Greek world were measured, is now mostly hidden beneath a railway line. A significant section of the altar was exposed in February 2011 during maintenance work and the altar briefly became the focus of protests (and a lawsuit) by archaeologists and local *dodekathístes* (Olympian god worshippers), who objected to the railway administration's plans to re-site its tracks atop the altar rather than prepare a diversion. However, a court ruled against them and the altar disappeared again in August 2011. Directly to its south, the outline of the **Altar of Ares** and **Temple of Ares** can be seen in gravel. Beyond them are the remains of the huge **Odeion of Agrippa**, a roofed theatre built in 15 BC. Before it are three gigantic statues of a god and two tritons.

The Stoa of Attalos

The eastern side of the Agora is dominated by the **Stoa of Attalos ⑯**. First erected by King Attalos II of Pergamon and

The reconstructed Stoa of Attalos in the ancient Greek Agora

opened in 138 BC, it was faithfully recreated during the 1950s, giving a stunning vision of what communal buildings were like in ancient times. Stoas were very popular in antiquity and all large settlements had at least one. These long colonnaded porches provided shade in summer and shelter in winter and were often used to link important community buildings. The Stoa of Attalos was a two-storey structure with small shops at the back. Today it houses the excavation offices and the excellent **Stoa of Attalos Museum**. Here you'll find a wide range of artefacts from the ancient Agora site, including six bronze ballots used in the deliberations of the *parabyston* or Court of the Eleven, concerned with criminal justice. Look out too for the *ostraka*, or clay tablets, bearing the names of those banished, or 'ostracised', from Athens for ten years – Hippokrates, Themistokles and Aristeides the Just being a few of the more famous exiles.

The 5th-century BC Hephaisteion

The Hephaisteion

The western side of the Agora is dominated by one of the best-preserved ancient Greek temples in the world, the **Hephaisteion**  (Temple of Hephaistos; also known, incorrectly, as the Theseion). The design of the temple, completed between 449 and 444 BC, is Doric mixed with Ionic elements. Hephaistos was the god of metallurgy, and this temple was set at the heart of the smithing, casting and ironmongery district. Later it was converted into the church of Ágios Geórgios with the addition of interior walls and a vaulted roof, surviving through Ottoman times – the last services were performed in 1834. It then served as a museum and storehouse.

The exterior of the temple is well preserved, reflecting the same building techniques as the Parthenon – without, however, *entasis*, making it seem clunky in comparison. The columns are more slender and the entablature (the space above the column capitals and below the pediments) sturdier. The metopes (square spaces, often carved in relief, between the triglyphs in a Doric frieze) on the entablature depict the legendary feats of Hercules and Theseus, the latter subject accounting for the long-standing misidentification of the temple.

South of the Hephaisteion along the paved path is an open area with a large reconstructed **site plan** displayed in a case. This gives a clear impression of what it looked like in AD 150.

The Tholos and Bouleuterion

Following the path through the Agora you'll see the round **Tholos** or **Prytaneion**, built in 465 BC as the assembly and dining hall for the *prytanes*, a governing committee responsible for the city's daily business. The 50 members of each tribal contingent took turns serving for approximately one month on this executive committee, and during this month they were fed at public expense in the Tholos. At night at least 17 members slept here so that decisions could be made in cases of emergency. Immediately north of the Tholos is the site of the original **Bouleuterion** (Council Chamber), constructed after

⊙ THE PANATHENAIC FESTIVAL

This important festival was made popular by Peisistratos (ruled 546–528 BC). It was held every four years in August, in honour of the goddess Athena. The festivities comprised athletic contests and musical events, and the winners were given vials containing olive oil from the fruit of the sacred groves of Athens. However, the most important element of the celebration was a procession that led from Kerameikos through the Agora along the Panathenaic Way (aka Sacred Way), finishing at the Parthenon, Athena's temple. At the head of the procession, on a wheeled ship propelled by priests and priestesses, was an embroidered garment to adorn the cult statue of Athena. This had been woven by the female guardians of the temple – the *Arrhephoroi*. Once within the sacred precincts, animal sacrifices were made before the statue was robed and the procession dispersed, but presumably festivities of some sort continued across the city for days afterwards.

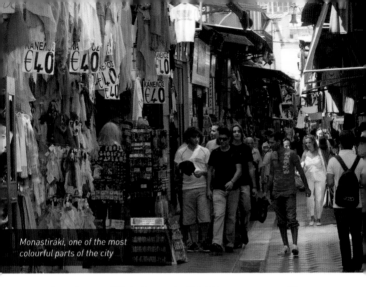
Monastiráki, one of the most colourful parts of the city

the reforms of Kleisthenes in 508 BC; most traces of it were erased when the currently visible **Metroön** (Temple of the Mother of the Gods) was erected here during the 2nd century BC, at the time that the **New Bouleuterion** was built just to the west.

MONASTIRÁKI

The area immediately northeast of the ancient Greek Agora is known as Monastiráki, one of the most colourful parts of Athens. South of Ermoú, which approximately bisects the district, mostly pedestrianised streets are full of pavement cafés, shops near the cathedrals selling religious articles, more overtly touristic boutiques selling ceramics, sandals and copper kitsch, and (centred on Platía Avyssinías) the used-furniture-and-metalware **flea market**, liveliest at weekends.

North of Ermoú lie more practical, workaday shops, especially in the sub-district of **Psyrrí** ⓲, which while past its heyday is still well colonised with tavernas, ouzeris and cafés. Ermoú itself forges east to Sýndagma Square (see page 62), with high-end retail outlets along the stretch to either side of a little square that's home to the beautiful 11th-century Byzantine church of **Kapnikaréa** ⓳. Many of its icons were painted during the 1950s by the Asia-Minor-born artist Fotis Kontoglou (1895–1965). Kapnikaréa was earmarked for demolition in the 1830s, but was saved by the personal intervention of Ludwig of Bavaria, father of Greece's first king.

MONASTIRÁKI SQUARE

The district revolves around **Monastiráki Square** (Platía Monastirakioú), always crowded with commuters hurrying to the Art Nouveau metro station, barrow-vendors of fruit and nuts, and itinerant peddlers of pirated films, watches and mobile phones. The originally 11th-century church at its centre – **Panagía Pandánassa** – was rebuilt in 1678 as the heart of a much larger convent, which has vanished. The south side of the square is dominated by the **Tzisdarákis Mosque** ⓴, built in 1759 by the Ottoman governor of the same name.

Just up Áreos from the mosque stands **Hadrian's Library** ㉑, built in AD 132 around a garden-courtyard with an ornamental pool. Only the west wall and a stretch of colonnade are now standing, but after years of desultory excavations the grounds are now partly open to the public (daily 8am–3pm).

Currently under construction, the **Museum of Greek Folk Art and Greek Folk Music Instruments** (www.melt.gr) is set to become the latest addition to the Monastiráki landscape. The new museum constitutes the merging and relocating of two Pláka museums to a site just north of the ancient Greek Agora:

the Museum of Greek Folk Art and the Museum of Greek Folk Music Instruments. The former offers an interesting collection of embroidery, lace and liturgical garments, as well as a wonderful array of paintings by the early 20th-century folk artist Theophilos Hatzimihail. Spinning and weaving are also represented, along with traditional puppets, festival masks and costumes. The Museum of Greek Folk Music Instruments will contribute its fascinating collection of instruments and musical recordings. The new, improved and comprehensive museum is due to open in 2018, on the block formed by Areos, Adrianou, Vrysakiou and Kladou streets.

BENAKI MUSEUM OF ISLAMIC ART

When the Benaki Museum (see page 66) was renovated in 2000 to focus on Greek history, all the fine Islamic art objects from the collection were moved to this excellent annexe, the **Museum of Islamic Art** ㉒ (Thu–Sun 10am–6pm; www.benaki. gr), in the Psyrrí district, at Agíon Asomáton 22. Here, two converted neoclassical mansions display over 8,000 items across four floors. They are presented roughly chronologically, and a map in each room shows the extent of the Islamic empire at that time. There are astronomical instruments, decorated rifles and daggers, illuminated manuscripts, dazzling ceramics, and many other breathtakingly beautiful objects. The ornate reception room from a Cairo mansion, re-created on the third floor, is a highlight.

HERAKLEIDON MUSEUM

Arguably the best of Athens' small, private museums is the **Herakleidon** ㉓ (Sun 10am–2pm; www.herakleidon-art.gr), a few steps west of the Hephaisteion, exploring the interrelationship between art, science, maths and philosophy. The core of the permanent collection is a large body of works by M C. Escher and Victor Vasarely, although the creation of a new interactive permanent exhibit encourages children and adults to consider links between science, art and maths through a series of clever interactive displays. Temporary exhibitions – in the recent past featuring Toulouse Lautrec and Edgar Degas – plus an exceptionally well-stocked shop are also compelling. A couple of minutes down the road, a new **annexe** (Apostolou Pavlou 37; daily 10am–6pm, Thu until 8pm), opened in 2014, is dedicated to art and culture, with some fascinating temporary exhibits.

KERAMEIKOS AND GÁZI

The most pleasant way to reach the archaeological site of **Kerameikos** ㉔ (Keramikós; daily 8am–3pm) on foot is not by following busy Ermoú which bounds it to the south, but by cutting through Psyrrí district, perhaps stopping for lunch at one of the tavernas just off its central Iróön Square. The archaeological site incorporates a section of the 478 BC city wall, and the Dipylos gate into Athens from Eleusis and Pireás.

Kerameikos funerary monument

The Panathenaic Procession (see page 51) would start from the separate, **Sacred Gate** here on its journey to the Acropolis, and the procession of the Eleusian Mysteries would leave the city via the same gate along the **Sacred Way**. The most important building found here, dating in its present version from Roman times, is the **Pompeion**, where procession paraphernalia was stored and where those involved would ready themselves.

Kerameikos was named after the potters who worked here within the city walls (Inner Kerameikos), on the site of good clay deposits along the banks of the River Eridanos (still flowing). Their work was transported around the Greek world, but the pots were not considered to be of any great value, designed to be used – and broken – within a year or so.

Outside the wall (Outer Kerameikos) was the major cemetery of the city (it was forbidden to bury the dead within the city walls), with burials dating from the 12th century BC. Major figures from Greek history were interred here, and their funerary monuments are some of the most exquisite items found during excavations around the city. The on-site **Oberlander Museum** (Tue–Sun 8am–3pm) exhibits burial finds dating from the 12th to 6th centuries BC.

For those whose artistic tastes lean more towards post-industrial landscapes, just beyond Kerameikos – across busy Pireós – is the old gas works of **Gázi**, with its round tank, stacks and warehouses: these have been converted into the **Tekhnópolis**, which hosts cultural events and exhibitions. Further down Pireós at no. 138, inside a converted ex-Lada dealership, is the city's premier temporary-exhibit venue: the multi-level **Benaki Museum Pireós Annexe** ㉕ (Thu, Sun 10am–6pm, Fri–Sat until 10pm; www.benaki.gr), featuring the best in contemporary painting, photography and installations, as well as an excellent snack bar. Recent top-notch exhibitions have included retrospectives of 20th-century Greek photographers Voula Papaioannou and Kostas Balafas, Belgian artist James Ensor, and Czech photographer Josef Koudelka.

OMÓNIA AND ENVIRONS

From Monastiráki, the parallel thoroughfares of Athinás and pedestrianised Eólou (more comfortable for walking) lead straight north to **Omónia Square** (Platía Omonías; Omónia means Concord), the apex of the traditional commercial triangle. Either street leads through the central market area, one of the most fascinating (and non-touristy) districts of Athens, where you can buy anything from live chipmunks to cinnamon sticks. Quieter Eólou offers, next to a little square with a flower market, the church of **Agía Iríni**, where superb chanting takes place on Sunday mornings.

Busier Athinás forges up to Evripídou with its spice stalls and the **Varvákio** ㉖, the 1870s-built meat-and-fish market on the right; the meat section works long hours, and also hosts several restaurants serving *patsás* (tripe soup), the traditional Greek hangover cure. Fruit and vegetables are sold on Platía Varvakíou to the left, and further on, at the edge of Psyrrí, lies Athens' **'Little Asia'**, full of Bangladeshi, Pakistani and Chinese shops. **Omónia Square**, when you finally reach it, proves anticlimactic, a constant race-track of traffic with little intrinsic interest.

The Mask of Agamemnon, National Archaeological Museum

THE NATIONAL ARCHAEOLOGICAL MUSEUM

A 10-minute walk north of Omónia along Patissíon brings you to the **National Archaeological Museum** 27 (Mon 1–8pm, Tue–Sun 9am–4pm; www.namuseum.gr), one of the world's most prestigious archaeological collections. Finds from numerous sites across the nation cover 7,000 years of Greek history, bringing the ancient Greek world to life by shedding light on almost every aspect of the citizens' daily activities. Devote at least a couple of hours to this amazing display, overhauled in phases from 2002 to 2005.

Directly ahead of you as you enter, the prehistoric collection (rooms 3–6) contains the treasure trove unearthed at Mycenae, including the exquisite gold **Mask of Agamemnon**. German-born archaeologist Heinrich Schliemann found the mask placed over the face of a body that he pronounced that of the legendary 13th-century BC King Agamemnon, but in fact it dates from more than 300 years earlier. In spite of this, the name remains. The prehistoric rooms also have a collection of Cycladic figures from the 3rd millennium BC. These simple, rounded female forms were funerary or devotional objects and are in contrast to the intricate pediment and frieze carvings and religious statuary from temples on the Acropolis. There is a rare male figure among the collection, and the beautiful **Harp Player** – a more complex carving in the same style.

Rooms 7–35 concentrate on sculpture – perhaps the greatest collection of ancient sculpture in the world – displayed to show the chronological development of the art form. Simple, idealised male and female figures (*kouroi* and *korai*) of the Archaic Age (mid-7th–5th century BC) give way to more ornate and literal human forms as you walk through the collection into the Classical Age and then on to the Hellenistic period followed by the Roman and Roman and Ptolemaic eras. Greek gods are well represented, as are various eminent human figures of Roman times, such as a bronze statue of the Roman emperor Augustus.

Room 15 is dominated by a fine statue of Poseidon in bronze (460 BC), found in the sea off the island of Évvia. The god is set to launch his trident against foes unknown. The Hall of the Stairs hosts another

The Jockey of the Artemision

statue dredged from the sea, the **Jockey of the Artemision**. The diminutive jockey rides a handsome steed which has its two front legs raised into the air, as if about to leap over an invisible obstacle.

Rooms 36 to 39 contain an extraordinary collection of bronzes, including votive offerings found at the Idaean Cave in Crete – mythical nursery of the god Zeus. Rooms 40 and 41 display artefacts from Egypt, especially from the Ptolemaic period when Ptolemy (a general under Alexander the Great, and therefore of Greek stock) took control of Egypt. One of his descendants was Queen Cleopatra.

The second-floor gallery with its famous 16th-century BC wall paintings from ancient Thera (modern Santoríni), depicting everyday scenes, is one of the highlights. The paintings show such detail and the colours so vivid it's astonishing to realise how old they are.

FROM OMÓNIA TO SÝNDAGMA

Three major thoroughfares – Stadíou, Panepistimíou and Aka-dimías – run parallel between the Omónia area and Sýndagma Square. The first two boulevards have up-market shops selling jewellery and designer labels, plus the giant Attica department store, and two modern stoas between them packed with more boutiques. These stoas were specifically mandated by the original Bavarian town plan of the 1830s and, aside from the surviving main-street grid, are its only aspect to have been faithfully adhered to.

At Paparigopoúlou 7 on the Sýndagma side of Platía Klávthmonos you'll find the **Museum of the City of Athens** ❷ (Mon, Wed–Fri 9am–4pm, Sat–Sun 10am–3pm; www.namuseum.gr), housed in King Otho's first residence when he arrived in Greece in 1832, with a model of Athens as it was a decade later. Nearer to Sýndagma, on Platía Kolokotróni, is the **National Historical Museum** (Tue–Sun 8.30am–2.30pm; free; www.nhmuseum.gr), lodged in what was Greece's original parliament building. Its collection focuses mostly on the 1820s Greek War of Independence and the personalities involved, most of

Subdued hues

The Hansen-designed Academy, National Library, and University are faithful reproductions of Classical architecture in all but one respect: colour. Flecks of paint on particularly well-preserved ancient artefacts tell us that neon-garish blues, reds, oranges and yellows were the rule for ancient statuary and relief work, but this was apparently felt to be too vulgar for modern sensibilities, so the pediments are in more subdued hues.

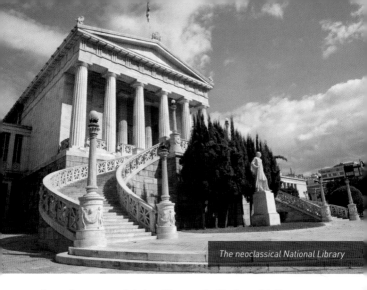
The neoclassical National Library

them shaggy mountain bandits recruited to the patriotic cause; an equestrian statue of one of them, Theodoros Kolokotronis, prances out front.

NEOCLASSICAL TRILOGY

Panepistimíou (University Street) is officially named Eleftheríou Venizélou after the Cretan-born statesman (though no one, not even official cartographers, calls it that). The location here of the **National Library**, the **University** and the **National Academy** ㉙ confirm it as the intellectual heart of modern Athens. All three neoclassical buildings give some idea of how the Agora of the ancient city may have looked in its prime.

The **Academy**, on which construction work began in 1859, is the most impressive of the three. It was designed by Theophilus von Hansen, a pre-eminent architect of his generation. The seated figures of Plato and Socrates guard the entrance and an intricately carved pediment depicts the birth of Athena; all were sculpted by Leonidas Drosos. A native of Denmark, Hansen was also responsible for the **National Library** (as well as the Royal Observatory in Athens and a number of buildings in Vienna). Hansen's brother Hans Christian designed the **University** in 1842; its portico, an attempted re-creation of the Parthenon's Propylaea, features frescoes of a seated King Otto flanked by the ancient Greek pantheon.

Continuing towards Sýndagma you will pass, at no. 12, the Ilíou Mélathron, once the home of Heinrich Schliemann and his wife Sophie. Today it houses the **Numismatic Museum** ③⓪ (Tue–Sun 9am–4pm; www.enma.gr), containing an extraordinary collection of 600,000 coins from antiquity to modern times.

Beyond the northeasternmost thoroughfare of Akadimías lies **Exárhia**, the traditional locus of book stores and book publishing, as well as being the student quarter, with multi-coloured graffiti and posters boosting every contrarian cause – plus periodic clashes between demonstrators and police.

SÝNDAGMA SQUARE AND AROUND

Platía Syndágmatos ③① (Constitution Square) is dominated on the west by the imposing facade of the **Parliament Building** (Voulí), originally built as the royal palace and completed in 1842. The west face, facing the square, has a Doric portico made of Pentelic marble. In front of the building on the retaining wall is the Memorial of the Unknown Soldier, commemorating all Greeks who have fallen in war. Decorated with a modern carved relief of a Classical theme, the marble is inscribed with an oration by Pericles honouring the

Sýndagma Square and the Parliament Building

Peloponnesian War dead. *Évzones* – traditionally dressed soldiers – guard the tomb and the presidential residence on Iródou Attikoú. The formal 'changing of the guard' takes place every Sunday at 10.45am; however, the *évzones* have a changeover daily on the hour, when two new guards take the place of the previous shift – something not to not miss on your trip to Athens.

The **Grande Bretagne Hotel** 32 on the northeast corner of the square was also built in 1842 as a sumptuous private residence and has become an Athenian institution. During World War II it served as the military headquarters of both the Germans and the British. Winston Churchill survived a thwarted bomb-plot here during his stay in December 1944. Thoroughly renovated before the 2004 Olympics, it is worth stopping in at the Grande Bretagne for a drink at the Alexander Bar (dress properly!).

The National Gardens

AROUND SÝNDAGMA

Just behind the Parliament building are the verdant landscaped grounds of the **National Gardens** ❸❸ (sunrise–sunset; free), conceived by King Otto's queen, Amalia, and an oasis with artificial streams and duck ponds. Just south of the garden is the **Záppeio** ❸❹, an imposing neoclassical building designed by Theophilus von Hansen as a national exhibition centre in 1878, set in its own gardens (24hr). It now houses a modern conference centre, with a popular (if pricey) café adjacent.

A five-minute stroll from Sýndagma along Amalías (or through the National Gardens) to the junction with Vassilísis Ólgas brings you to **Hadrian's Arch** ❸❺, built by the Athenians for the emperor Hadrian in AD 131–32. The west side of the arch facing the Acropolis and the ancient agoras bears an inscription reading, 'This is Athens, the former city of Theseus'. The inscription on the other side reads 'This is the city of Hadrian and not of Theseus'.

Immediately southeast looms the **Temple of Olympian Zeus** ❸❻ (Stíles Olymbíou Dioú; daily 8am–3pm), the largest temple ever built on Greek soil. Work began on this colossal temple in the 6th century BC, but was only completed 650 years later. Hadrian dedicated the temple to the ruler of the ancient pantheon, Zeus Olympios, during the Panathenaic Festival in AD

131–32. It was imperative that the temple should be fitting for his position, and its dimensions – 96m (315ft) long and 40m (130ft) wide, with columns more than 17m (53ft) high – are truly majestic. Originally 104 columns surrounded an inner sanctum that protected a gold-and-ivory statue of Zeus which has since been lost. Today only 16 columns are still standing, but their Corinthian capitals have a wonderful form and elegance.

The temple sat close to the banks of the River Ilissos in ancient times and near the fountain of Kallirrhoe, whose lush vegetation created an even more beautiful vista. Today the river has been covered over and lies beneath busy Kaliróis boulevard. Nearby, where Vassilísis Ólgas meets Vassiléos Konstandínou, is the **Kallimármaro Stadium** ㉗, sitting in the lee of Ardittós Hill, and first constructed in 330–329 BC for the ancient Panathenaic Games. It was rebuilt by the city's great benefactor, Herodes Atticus, in AD 140. A modern Greek benefactor, George Averoff, sponsored the stadium's reconstruction for the first modern Olympic Games, held here in 1896. However, the length is too short and the turns too tight for modern athletic events, so the 2004 Olympic Games were held primarily at OAKA, a purpose-built Olympic complex in the northern suburb of Maroússi.

Lykavitós

Northeast of Sýndagma rises the steep, pine-covered hill of Lykavitós, which unlike Filopáppos and Ardittós was not settled in ancient times owing to a lack of water supply. Today it is topped by the chapel of Ágios Geórgios and a rather overpriced restaurant. Both can be reached either by an arduous walk up from the posh Kolonáki residential district at the foot of the hill, or by the funicular from the corner of Aristíppou and Ploutárhou (9am–3am daily; at least half-hourly).

At the summit of Lykavitós Hill

VASSILÍSIS SOFÍAS MUSEUMS

Vassilísis Sofías, the main thoroughfare leading east from Sýndagma, passes several major embassies – and several important museums, some a bit closer to the Evangelismós metro station.

Closest to Sýndagma is the **Theoharakis Foundation for Fine Arts and Music** ㉘ (daily 10am–6pm, Oct–May Thu until 8pm, closed Aug; www.thf.gr) at no. 9, corner Mérlin, with a changing programme of exhibitions and small chamber concerts. Next up is the **Benaki Museum** ㉙ (Koumbári 1; Wed and Fri 9am–5pm, Thu and Sat until midnight, Sun until 3pm; free Thu; www.benaki.gr), a collection donated to the state in 1954 by the wealthy cotton merchant Emmanouil Benakis, who was born in the Greek community of Alexandria. It is probably the only museum that covers all ages of Greek culture and history, and there are Greek works of art from prehistoric to modern times. There is also an excellent gift shop and a very popular rooftop café.

Three blocks over from Sýndagma stands the **Museum of Cycladic Art** ㊵ (Mon, Wed, Fri–Sat 10am–5pm, Thu until 8pm, Sun 11am–5pm; www.cycladic.gr). Permanent exhibits highlight the exquisite marble figurines discovered in the Cyclades islands (c.3000–2000 BC). Most of these are female, suggesting the worship of fertility or an earth-mother religion. The museum is lately becoming renowned for completely unrelated but excellent temporary exhibits – anything from El Greco and his school, to Eros in antiquity.

Further down Vassilísis Sofías at no. 22 is the 2004-extended **Byzantine and Christian Museum** ❹ (Tue–Sun 9.30am–5.30pm; www.byzantinemuseum.gr). One of the original buildings here is a splendid 19th-century mansion built for the eccentric Philhellene Duchesse de Plaisance (1785–1854), who was married to one of Napoleon's associates but came to Greece, fell in love with the country, and stayed. The mansion is no longer used for exhibits; the bulk of the artefacts, from the early Christian period right through to 13th-century Attica, are found in a huge and impressive modern underground wing. Despite being subterranean the galleries are light and spacious, and the items (including the 7th-century Hoard of Mytilene) well-displayed and informatively labelled. This stylish transformation has made what was once a small and specialist collection into one of the major Athens museums.

Next door is the **War Museum** ❷ (daily Apr–Oct 9am–7pm, Nov–Mar until 5pm; www.warmuseum.gr), established during the 1967–74 dictatorship. Outside stand various 20th-century artillery and aeroplanes, while the interior offers a surprisingly absorbing collection of uniforms, weaponry and documents (scantily labelled in English), particularly good on Greece's tribulations during World War II – though omitting the still-controversial civil war.

Opposite Evangelismós metro station and the Hilton Hotel is the **National Gallery** ❸ (closed for expansion and renovation until further notice; www.nationalgallery.gr). The core collection of Greek art from just before independence to recent years does a good job of placing it in social context and as part of international trends. Few of the artists except Nikos-Hatzikyriakos Ghikas (Ghika) are household names overseas, but that's no reflection on their merit. The best modern piece has to be Fotis Kontoglou's mural, which adorned his own house.

EXCURSIONS

Athens is undeniably a fascinating city, but with the traffic and congestion, even the listed attractions can begin to pall after a few days. Luckily you are perfectly placed to take in numerous excursions for the day or even a few days, either on an organised tour or under your own steam.

MONASTERY OF KESSARIANÍ

Nestled in a vale on the slopes of Mount Ymittós 5km (3 miles) east of the city centre, the **monastery of Kessarianí** ❹ (Tue–Sun 8.30am–3pm) and its surrounding gardens are a favourite retreat of city-dwellers. The River Ilissos rises here, nourishing the vegetation which has been a constant since ancient times; gently graded hiking trails loop through the gardens and further into the wilderness of Pendéli. The monastery compound itself encloses a refectory, Byzantine baths and the original 11th-century church, decorated with vivid frescoes from 1682 of scenes from the life of Christ.

MONASTERY OF DAFNÍ

The ancient Sacred Way or Ierá Odós (see page 51) – now traced more or less exactly by the modern boulevard of the same name – heads west from Kerameikos to the edge of the city, in Haïdári district. Here in a wooded pass, 10km (6 miles) from the centre, sits the **Monastery of Dafní** ❺ (Tue and Fri 8am–3pm; free), built on the site of an earlier temple of Apollo.

The monastery seen today dates from about 1070; from 1207 until 1458, when Athens was ruled by Frankish lords,

Cistercian monks lived here. Reoccupation of the monastery by Orthodox monks resumed only during the early 16th century, but they were expelled during the 1820s for harbouring independence fighters. Restoration took place twice after World War II, and yet again since 1999 when the last Athens earthquake caused severe damage. The pretty Byzantine church is renowned for its beautiful mosaics, particularly that of *Christ Pantokrator* in the main dome.

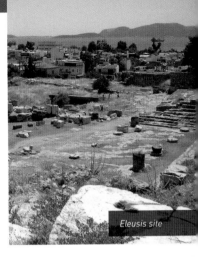
Eleusis site

ANCIENT ELEUSIS

Continuing along the Sacred Way, which in ancient times was lined with shrines and tombs, brings you to an industrial landscape of shipyards, steel foundries and oil refineries on the Saronic Gulf – amidst which, incongruously, is one of antiquity's most hallowed sites: **Eleusis** ⓰ (daily 8am–3pm, until 8pm in summer), marooned beside decidedly unromantic modern Elefsína.

Eleusis was home to the Sanctuary of Demeter and the Eleusian Mysteries – a series of complex and enigmatic rituals performed by priests before an audience of male, non-slave citizens. The Mysteries thrived from the Mycenaean to the Christian eras, but the exact nature of the rites was never divulged, as all initiates kept – on pain of death – the secrets of the cult. Eleusis has suffered badly over the centuries, and the excellent site museum with finds and models of the sanctuary helps make sense of what today is largely an expanse of jumbled masonry.

BRAURON (VRAVRÓNA)

Some 4km (2.5 miles) east of the airport, but reached along a roundabout road via Markópoulo, lies the evocative sanctuary of **Brauron** 47 (Vravróna; Tue–Sun 8am–3pm), sacred to Artemis and one of the earliest such shrines, supposedly established here by Agamemnon's daughter Iphigeneia. Another legend holds that, in atonement for slaying one of Artemis' sacred bears, the nobility of Attica were required to dedicate their young daughters as novices ('little bears') of the goddess; the 2010-revamped site **museum**, 1.5km (1 mile) further (same hours), is full of small-girl figurines holding various live offerings to the goddess, or dressed in bear-masks. The green site itself, watered by a still-flowing sacred spring, features the 5th-century BC **Stoa of the Little Bears**, what remains of the hostel for the young novices.

Bronze gods

Just northwest of Zéa is the Archaeological Museum of Piraeus (Tue–Sun 8.30am–3pm), a rather dour building hiding a wealth of artefacts found during local excavations – or dredged by chance from the sea bed nearby. Pride of place goes to a 6th-century BC life-sized bronze of Apollo, displayed along with similar statues of Artemis and Athena.

SOÚNIO

The peninsula of southern Attica extends into the Aegean Sea, and at Soúnio – its most windswept tip – the ancient Greeks built a beautiful **Temple of Poseidon** 48 (daily 9am–sunset, from 9.30am in winter), god of the sea, earthquakes and horses. The views from here are beautiful whatever the time of day – but the sunsets are particularly spectacular. The

Piraeus Zéa marina

temple itself is one of the finest in Greece. Of the original 34 Doric columns only 16 are still in situ, and the ornate frieze on the pediment and entablature has been ravaged by the salty air, but the whole effect of the building combined with the setting – a sandy beach on one side and a sheer drop on the other – is magnificent.

Sounion is reached by following the coast road from the capital 70km (43 miles) southeast through several resort-suburbs with both fee-payable and free beaches.

PIRAEUS

Just 10km (6 miles) southwest of Athens, and almost indistinguishable from the sprawling capital, is **Piraeus** (Piréas) ㊾, actually the fourth-largest city in Greece, and the country's largest container port. Although most people just use Piraeus as a departure point for the islands, there are a few attractions. Coming from central Athens, the metro brings you to within walking distance of the numerous distinct quays or *aktés* accommodating swarms of ferries, catamarans and hydrofoils. From Aktí Miaoúli any street heading south leads to pretty **Zéa marina** (formerly Pasálimani), the second of Piraeus' three natural harbours, crammed with enormous pleasure craft and smaller yachts. Aktí Moutsopoúlou, lined with expensive fish restaurants, loops around the bay. Still further east is **Mikrolímano**, home to more boats and pleasant cafés.

THE SARONIC GULF ISLANDS

The islands closest to Athens are those of the Saronic Gulf: Égina (Aegina), Póros, Ýdra (Hydra) and Spétses. Hydrofoils for these islands depart from Aktí Miaoúli at Piraeus, slower ferries just opposite from Aktí Posidónos. Note that there are very few connections between Égina and the other islands. At busy times like Sunday evening, all sea-craft back towards Piraeus sell out, so buy a return ticket or see to it immediately upon arrival.

Égina (Aegina)

On the closest island to the mainland, just 45 minutes distant by hydrofoil, the pretty quayside of **Égina (Aegina) town**, with its neoclassical buildings, awaits as you disembark near the whitewashed chapel of Ágios Nikólaos, protecting the harbour entrance. Walk along the water's edge past the colourful fishing fleet, have lunch at a taverna in the marketplace or buy some of the pistachio nuts for which the island is renowned. Égina is a delight out of season, but can be very busy on warm weekends; many wealthy Athenian families have second homes here. The resort of **Agía Marína** is 15km (9 miles) from the town on the east coast and has a good, child-friendly beach. Just before, stop off at the 5th-century BC **Temple of Aphaea**, set on a hilltop amidst pines.

Póros

The volcanic double-island of Póros lies less than 150m (465ft) from the Greek mainland, off the northeastern coast of the Argolid Peninsula and an hour from Piraeus by hydrofoil or sea-Cat. Small sailing boats throng the narrow straits, a summertime yachtsman's paradise. **Póros town** – the only settlement on the island – is a maze of narrow winding streets rising up a small hill with a clock tower. The seafront is the hub of all activity, with tavernas and cafés lining the waterside. The rest of Póros, called Kalávria, is covered with verdant pine forest, while the coastline is dotted with small pebbly coves – great for swimming and snorkelling, but crowded.

Póros harbour

The only other sights, both on Kalávria, are the **Monastery of Zoödóhou Pigís**, above the island's best beach, and the foundations of a **Poseidon temple** well inland near the top of the island. Here the famous Greek orator Demosthenes chose suicide in 322 BC rather than surrender to Macedonian forces.

Ýdra (Hydra)

Just over an hour and a half from Athens by hydrofoil or catamaran, Ýdra (Hydra) is the most celebrated of the Saronic Gulf islands, and the approach into its harbour the most dramatic. The beautiful port of **Ýdra Town** remains hidden until the very last moment, and when the panorama comes into view your camera should be ready. Above the narrow cove the hillsides are blanketed with neoclassical mansions. There are no cars on Ýdra except for the odd rubbish truck and mechanical digger, only donkeys which transport almost everything up the slopes. There are few beaches, but the water is generally clear, and there is some excellent walking.

Still, most people don't visit Ýdra for any activity other than to 'see and be seen'. During the 1950s and 1960s the island was an artist colony, prior to becoming an upscale resort and cruise call. Pricey jewellery boutiques intermingle with craft galleries, exclusive restaurants, surprisingly inexpensive tavernas and chic cafés.

Spétses
At well over two hours away from Piraeus, **Spétses** is the remotest of the Saronic Gulf islands and just a bit too far to do as a day-trip. The town, while not as immediately striking as Ýdra's, has a similar architecture and straggles pleasantly along the north coast for several kilometres. Unlike Ýdra, motorised vehicles are not totally banned on Spétses, though private cars are prohibited in the town itself – horse-drawn buggies, scooters and a few conventional taxis are the main alternatives. Away from town, Spétses has the best beaches and cleanest water of any Saronic Gulf island, easily explored by hired boat or scooter.

THE ARGOLID PENINSULA
The history of ancient Greece is punctuated with the feats of city-states led by great leaders, of which Athens is, of course, the most famous. Within a day's journey of the capital lies the **Argolid Peninsula**, a region of the Peloponnese where the sites of two such city-states – Corinth and Mycenae – can be viewed. Those with more time should definitely visit the ancient Theatre of Epidauros and the port city of Návplio.

The Corinth Canal

An engineering marvel, the **Corinth Canal** cuts the narrow isthmus that links the Peloponnese with the Greek mainland and divides the Saronic and Corinth gulfs. Sailing around the Peloponnese took considerable time and exposed ships to some of the most dangerous waters in the Mediterranean – especially in winter. Ancient Greeks ported their huge vessels

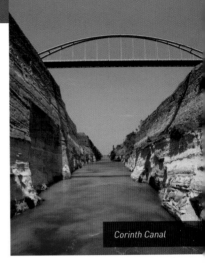

Corinth Canal

across the 6km (4-mile) wide isthmus, and as early as AD 67, the Roman Emperor Nero was making the first attempts at cutting a canal. It would not become a reality until 1893 when, after 11 years of digging, a channel was opened for shipping. Its modest dimensions, however, made it obsolete almost immediately, even more so in the contemporary era of supertankers. Today it is used mostly by yachts – and bungy-jumpers, who launch themselves from the pedestrian catwalk below the road bridge (June–Aug Wed–Sun 10am–5.45pm, May & Sept–Oct Sat–Sun only) courtesy of Zulu Bungy (www.zulubungy.com).

Ancient Corinth

In ancient times Corinth rivalled Athens for power and influence. It mimicked the layout of the larger city – a town radiating out from the base of a rocky promontory which supported a temple of Aphrodite – though Acrocorinth is far higher and larger than the Acropolis.

Corinth was an active and prosperous city from the 8th to the 5th centuries BC, founding many colonies and competing fiercely with Athens; it sided with Sparta against Athens during the Peloponnesian Wars. During the Hellenistic period the city was economically prosperous despite political instability. After 224 BC when the Achaean League was formed, Corinth became a centre of independent Greek political life. This brought it into direct conflict with Rome, which razed Corinth to the ground in 146 BC.

The site was unoccupied for just over 100 years, until Julius Caesar began to rebuild the city in 44 BC; revitalised, Corinth soon became the capital of the Roman province of Achaea.

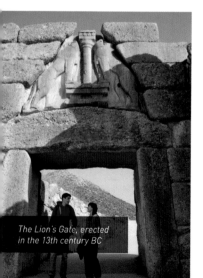

The Lion's Gate, erected in the 13th century BC

The city developed its two ports (Kenchreai to the east and Lechaion to the west of the isthmus) and was flourishing when St Paul arrived on his first visit to Corinth in AD 50/51, when he successfully established a community of believers.

During the 3rd and 4th centuries Corinth suffered attacks by the Goths and a major earthquake in 375. The 6th century saw another earthquake and Slavic raids, after which the city was abandoned.

The modern, uninteresting city of Corinth lies several kilometres northeast of **ancient Corinth** (May–Sept 8am–8pm, Oct until 6 or 7pm, Nov–Apr until 3pm). Most prominent as you approach the site is the Doric **Temple of Apollo**, built in the 6th century BC and one of the oldest buildings in Corinth. Many other remains date from the Roman era, including ornate facades of the **Fountain of Peirene**, where you can still hear the waters flowing through cavities at the rear, and the **Lechaion Way**, with worn cart tracks clearly visible in the marble slabs.

The **Bema** (platform), traditionally believed to be where St Paul stood before the Roman consul, is situated to the south side of the agora. The site **museum** contains some interesting finds and features a number of dioramas depicting Corinth as it would once have looked.

After visiting the ancient city, head uphill to take in the magnificent site of **Acrocorinth** (daily 8am–3pm). Fortified since the 7th century BC, the summit is still encircled by high masonry walls continually reinforced during the Byzantine, Frankish, Venetian and Ottoman eras. At the summit, within three layers of protective walls, are the remains of a Temple of Aphrodite, an early Christian basilica, Byzantine cisterns, a Frankish tower, the upper Peirene spring plus Ottoman mosques and hamams.

Nemea

Some 19km (12 miles) further down the motorway from ancient Corinth, ancient **Nemea** (daily 8am–3pm) is well worth the short detour west. A sanctuary rather than a town, its highlight is a massive Doric Temple of Nemean Zeus which you are free to walk completely around; nine of its columns have been re-erected by the Californian excavators. A good site museum and stadium 1km (0.6 miles) north, with the oldest entrance tunnel known, round out the attractions.

Mycenae

From the 15th to the 11th century BC, this rocky outcrop was one of the most important centres in the known world, seat of the mighty Mycenaean empire which grew to encompass mainland Greece and most Aegean islands. The exploits of the Mycenaeans, and their greatest leader Agamemnon, were thought to be myth until – in the 1870s – archaeologist Heinrich Schliemann set out to find evidence of Homer's stories in (until then) strictly legendary Troy and Mycenae. He successfully uncovered both sites, and thereby transformed the world of archaeology – and man's view of history.

Schliemann found the remains of the city of **Mycenae** (Mykínes; daily May–Oct 8am–8pm, April until 7pm, Nov–Mar until 3pm) buried under millennia of debris in a sheltered valley some 60km (37 miles) south of Corinth. It was so well hidden that the site had been completely forgotten.

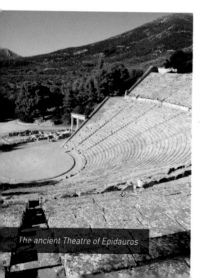

The ancient Theatre of Epidauros

The military might of the Mycenaeans had been well documented by Homer, but nothing could prepare Schliemann's team for the artistic treasures unearthed here. As they dug through the remains, the tombs of several royal personalities were discovered; each skeleton lay where it had been carefully buried, its face covered in a mask of pure gold. Exquisite statuary and intricate jewellery found in the family tombs below show a softer side of these enigmatic people and bring the world of Agamemnon to life. All the artefacts from the site were taken to Athens, many now displayed in the National Archaeological Museum (see page 58).

Mycenae's massive **Cyclopean walls** – huge, rough-hewn masonry blocks laid atop one another with extreme precision, and without mortar – are so called because later Hellenes could not believe that humans were responsible for the construction and so gave the credit to the one-eyed giant of myth. The outer walls date from around 1250 BC; they surround and protect the citadel through which the only entrance is the **Lion's Gate**, decorated with the earliest known monumental sculpture in Europe.

Just beyond the gate, look down to the right to see **Grave Circle A**, where the royal graves were found, then climb to the summit remains of the Royal Palace, from where the views of the surrounding countryside are superb. Outside the walls are three *tholos* (beehive) tombs, including the **Treasury of Atreus**, otherwise known as the **Tomb of Agamemnon**, constructed in about 1330 BC. The masonry – again eschewing the use of mortar – is superb.

Epidauros

Southeast of Mycenae, some 40 minutes' drive via Návplio, is another ancient site also renowned for its acoustics. The extraordinarily well-preserved **Theatre of Epidauros** (Epídavros; daily May–Oct 8am–8pm, April until 7pm, Nov–Mar until 5pm) was built in the late 4th century BC and could accommodate an audience of 12,000 people. It has startling acoustics: you may not hear the proverbial pin drop in the centre of the stage while you are sitting in an upper row, but you can certainly hear quiet speech. Performances are staged here every summer, as part of the **Athens and Epidauros Festival** (see page 84). The theatre was part of a much larger **Sanctuary of Asklepion**, one of the most important centres of healing in the ancient world.

Návplio

The beautiful port town of **Návplio** makes the perfect base for touring the region. Set on the south coast of the Argolid, it has been a strategic strongpoint for centuries and has no less than three interlocking castles dating from Byzantine and Venetian times on the towering rock of Palamídi, plus a fourth on the rock of Akronavplía. The city retains much of its Venetian and Ottoman past in the form of impressive churches and mosques.

Formal attractions include an **archaeological museum** (Tue–Sun 8am–3pm) in a former Venetian barracks, with finds from all the local sites, and the excellent **Peloponnesian Folklore Foundation** (Mon–Sat 9am–2.30pm, Sun 9.30am–3pm; www.pli.gr). The seaside promenade has locals and Athenians alike strolling in the evening. Look out towards the tiny fortified island of **Boúrtzi**; the Venetian castle there has variously been the residence of the town's executioner and a luxury hotel.

DELPHI

The advice of the oracle at **Delphi** (Delfí; daily 8am–3pm) was available to all who were willing to make the pilgrimage to the Sanctuary of Apollo, nowadays a three-hour journey on a modern road from Athens, on the flanks of Mount Parnassós.

In ancient times Delphi was the spiritual centre of the Greek world, and no important decisions of state were made without consulting the oracle here. The cult flourished from the 8th century BC to the 4th century AD. The resident priestess or *Pythia* sat inside the Temple of Apollo, periodically falling into a trance when Apollo would enter her as his medium. Her unintelligible mutterings were interpreted by temple priests, who in turn would give often ambiguous answers to the supplicants.

A modern road cuts through the ancient remains, and the approach to the site from the parking area leads up a sacred way, past many treasuries and offerings dedicated by various city-states, to the magnificent **Temple of Apollo**, largely reconstructed by French archaeologists. About 400m (1,300ft) east are the waters of the **Kastalian Spring**, where pilgrims would purify themselves before consulting the Pythia. Just below the road and the spring are the remains of a large gymnasium used by athletes competing in the Pythian

The Tholos, Delphi

Games, and the temple of **Athena Pronaia**, where pilgrims would make their first religious stop on the climb to the sanctuary. The most impressive building at this lower site, of uncertain function, is the circular **Tholos**, built in mottled stone. The local **museum** (daily 9am–4pm) displays an extraordinary collection of statuary and other artefacts found at the site, the most famous exhibit being the 5th-century BC bronze statue of the **Charioteer**. Other items include two enormous 6th-century BC *kouroi*, and a life-sized votive bull fashioned from hammered silver and copper.

ÓSIOS LOUKÁS MONASTERY

Located 35km (22 miles) southwest of Delphi, the **Monastery of Ósios Loukás** (daily summer 10am–5pm, winter 8am–3pm) is one of the finest Byzantine buildings in the country. Mosaics in the 11th-century church are rivalled in Greece only by those at Dáfni, Néa Moní on Híos, and a few in Thessaloníki.

Athens' vibrant nightlife

WHAT TO DO

ENTERTAINMENT

Athens comes alive after dark with a range of activities; however, you'll probably need to alter your normal routine to enjoy it as locals do. Theatre or cinema performances are followed by a late, leisurely dinner, often after 11pm, and musical club performances begin at around midnight. Even if you only want to sample the delights of Greek tavernas, the real atmosphere accrues after 9pm.

For most Greeks, the traditional taverna – eating, drinking and often singing with friends – is still the favoured choice for a night out. Other options include trendy bars (barákia), especially in Psyrrí, Gázi, Roúf, Keramikós and Metaxourgío districts; live venues with jazz, Greek music or rock; dance clubs with a techno, house or ambient soundtrack; and musical tavernas where food prices reflect the live entertainment.

THEATRE, CINEMA AND MUSIC

The ancient Greeks were credited with inventing drama and comedy, and this tradition carries on into the present. The city has dozens of active **theatres** at peak winter times, though the season lasts from October to May, and you might make a special effort to see a play in the magnificent theatre at Epidauros (see page 79). All performances are in Greek. From late May to mid-September, **open-air cinemas** (theriná) operate in most neighbourhoods. Screenings are typically at 9pm and 11pm (8.30pm and 10.30pm in September), and films – usually from the preceding winter – are subtitled, with the original soundtrack. The best programmed and most central are the

Thiseion near the Acropolis, the Zephyros in Petrálona district, the Riviera and Vox in Exárhia, and the Athinaia and Dexameni in Kolonáki; there's a full list at www.athensinfoguide.com/nl cinemas.htm.

From October to May a full programme of classical music and some dance and jazz is at the **Mégaro Mousikís** (Athens Concert

⊙ SUMMER FESTIVALS

The **Athens and Epidauros Festival** currently runs from June through early August only, owing to funding restrictions, and features choral concerts, dance and recitals. Tickets are fairly priced. Since 1955 performances have been staged at the atmospheric open-air **Herodes Atticus** theatre below the Acropolis, with world-class performers both foreign and Greek; more recently the **Mégaron Mousikís**, a venue at **Pireós 260** and the **small amphitheatre at Paleá Epídavros** have handled nearly as many events. On weekend nights during July and early August the **main ancient theatre of Epidauros** stages ancient Greek plays presented in modern Greek. Transport is laid on to the last two.

For information and tickets concerning all festival productions, go online (www.greekfestival.gr) or ring general information (tel: 210 92 82 900). Alternatively, visit the main box office at Panepistimíou 39, in the arcade (Mon–Sat); the Herodes Atticus box office on the day of the performance (9am–2pm and 6–9pm); or the box office at ancient Epidauros (Mon–Thu 9am–7pm, Fri–Sat 9am–9pm). Be warned that big-name events sell out quickly.

Sadly, the long-established **Vyronas Festival** has become a casualty of hard times. But the July **Rematia Festival** at the Evripideio Theatre in Halándri (www.theatrorematias.gr) continues, with everything from Colombian accordion bands to Greek theatre.

Theatre of Herodes Atticus

Hall; tel: 210 72 82 333; www.megaron.gr). The **Lyriki Skini** or national opera company in the Olympia Theatre (Akadimías 59–61; www.nationalopera.gr) has opera, ballet and operetta.

TRADITIONAL MUSIC AND DANCE

Greece has a rich legacy of folk dance and music; however genuine, spontaneous performances are hard to find in the capital. From late May to late September the **Dóra Strátou Folk Dance Theatre** stages traditional Greek song, dance and music in its own open-air theatre below the Filopáppos monument, in Petrálona (daily except Mon/Tue; for details see www.grdance.org/en/).

SPORTS

Athens' proximity to the coast allows you to combine **beach activities** with a city holiday, with some excellent facilities within a 40-minute taxi or bus ride of the centre. You'll find a full range of sports on offer, from tennis, windsurfing and waterskiing to snorkelling and scuba. However, the nearby submarine world can be disappointing, and the water is not generally considered clean enough for bathing anywhere north of Glyfáda.

Much of Athens closes down during August (though not those businesses relating to tourism), when people head to the coast, the mountains or the islands. **Beaches** are busy throughout the school holidays, approximately from 11 June to 8 September. The closest resort to the centre is **Glyfáda**, only 12km (7 miles) away. About 20km (12 miles) distant is **Voúla**, a bit less crowded than Glyfáda. **Vouliagméni** is 5km (3 miles) further south, while **Várkiza** lies another 5km (3 miles) further still, at the end of city bus lines. There are some luxurious hotels in both Voúla and Vouliagméni, and each of these resorts has at least one beach with changing facilities, food and watersports. An entrance fee of about €5 is typical. You'll find cleaner, free sandy beaches at **Anávysos**, **Saronída** and **Soúnio**, accessible by KTEL Attikís buses rather than urban lines.

The **Saronic Gulf islands** have a longer season, from May to October, owing to foreigner patronage. Égina (Aegina) does not have the best sea; you may prefer its little satellite Angístri for swimming. Póros, Ýdra and Spétses generally have clean water and are the best organised for watersports.

SAILING

Summer **sailing** is very popular with Athenians, as regular regattas and the crowded marinas at Piraeus, Álimos and Glyfáda all testify. Several companies hire boats with crew, or 'bare' if you have a skipper's certificate. Try, for example, Fyly Yachting and Partners at Posidónos 73, Paleó Fáliro (tel: 210 98

58 670; www.fyly.gr), or MG
Yachts, Makáriou 2 corner
Posidónos, Kalamáki (tel:
210 98 59 101; www.mg
yachts.gr).

SKIING

The closest skiing facilities can be found at **Mount
Parnassós** (see page 58),
nearly three hours' drive
from the city, where there
are 20 or so mostly inter-
mediate runs open from
December to April, weather
(especially high winds) per-

Swimming in the west of Ýdra

mitting. The hotels and tavernas of modern Delfí and Aráhova
lie 20 minutes from the slopes. Aráhova is also full of outfitters
for renting or buying equipment; these – and lift passes – are
comparable in cost to that of the Alps or Pyrenees.

FOOTBALL (SOCCER)

Football is a national obsession in Greece, and Athens' first-
division (Superleague) teams (Panathinaïkós, AEK, Panionios
and Atrómitos), plus Olympiakós of Piraeus, feature promi-
nently in domestic and European competition. The season runs
from September to May, with matches on Wednesday nights
and Saturday afternoons. Both AEK and Panathinaïkós play at
the OAKA facility in Maroússi until or unless new home stadi-
ums are built for them. Olympiakós' Karaïskáki stadium is in
Néo Fáliro, at the end of one tram line. Ask hotel reception for
assistance in obtaining match tickets.

Shoe shopping in Athens

SHOPPING

Athens offers abundant shopping opportunities, not only for typical Greek-style souvenirs, but for haute couture, art and jewellery. Whatever your budget, you are bound to find something exciting to take home – whether a mass-produced item or a unique hand-finished piece. Individual districts specialise in certain types of goods.

WHERE TO SHOP

For undeniably tacky, mass-produced kitsch, head for **Pláka**, where such outlets are interspersed with galleries, t-shirt shops and numerous street hawkers selling novelty toys or handmade budget art. The warren of streets around the cathedral offers religious souvenirs – *thymiatíria* (incense burners), icons and *támata* (votive offerings) being the most portable.

Monastiráki is Athens' old bazaar area; at the Saturday/Sunday **flea market** on and around Platía Avyssinías (see page 52) you can find old metalware, dishes, memorabilia and furniture, while an array of small shops on Iféstou sells everything from used CDs and beads to army-surplus-type clothing. The covered **Varvákio market** (see page 57) between Athinás and Eólou offers a range of packaged Greek foodstuffs to take home.

The **Kolonáki** district is an Athenian favourite for boutiques and home-furnishing stores selling the best of European design; prices match (and sadly sometimes exceed) quality here. Ermoú, Eólou and Stadíou streets are where you will find more middle-of-the-road shops selling everything from shoes and clothing to household wares. There are also Greek department stores such as Attica, inside the Citylink complex between Stadíou and Panepistimíou (www.atticadps.gr), Fokas (Ermoú 11 corner Voulís) and Notos Home Galleries (Platía Kotziá, corner Eólou; www.notoshome.gr).

WHAT TO BUY

Copper and brassware. Copper and brass have long been used for household utensils, and skilled craftsmen still work in small, central workshops. Newly made goods have a bright patina that mellows with age; some of the older pieces – including water ewers, bowls and covered pilaf vessels – are exceptionally beautiful. Ornate Ottoman-style trays (*siniá*) set on folding wooden bases will just fit in your luggage, as will serving ladles and goats' bells. The best sources of antique copperware are several shops at the far end of Adrianoú opposite the Stoa of Attalos, and stalls on Platía Avyssinías. New copperware is sold at a few shops on Iféstou. None of it is especially cheap, but hard bargaining at slow times can yield fair prices.

Ceramics. Exquisite hand-thrown and painted copies of ancient pieces are available at a price, though you can also buy less expensive factory-produced items. Traditionally shaped urns, jugs and cups are decorated with scenes depicting the lives of ancient mortals or the Greek gods. Modern ceramic artists also thrive, showcased in various small galleries.

Statuary. If you want a (licit) little piece of ancient Greece then you will have no trouble finding your own reproduction copy of a deity or a Classical statue. Plaques depicting ancient friezes or masks to hang on walls are also extremely popular, as are Mycenaean helmets.

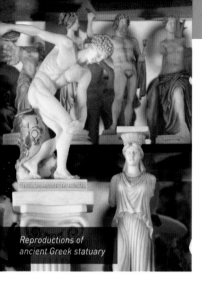
Reproductions of ancient Greek statuary

If Classical statuary is too ornate for your taste, then copies of the minimalist Cycladic idols are to be found at the Museum of Cycladic Art. Similarly, both the Benaki Museum and National Archaeological Museum offer high-quality copies of items from their collection. Each comes with a certificate of authentication.

Leatherware. Goat- and cow-hides are worked into a range of footwear, bags and clothing, though quality is generally more rustic and bohemian than similar items produced in Italy or France.

Carpets and needlepoint. The carpet-weaving tradition was largely introduced by Asia Minor refugees. Look for hand-knotted ornate patterns in wool or silk, which come with a hefty price tag. Hand-produced *flokáti* rugs made from sheep hides were used in farmhouses on the mainland.

Needlepoint, crochet and embroidery – once activities undertaken by every Greek woman – are dying arts, so any hand-crafted pieces will become collectors' items. Machine-produced pieces are readily available as tablecloths, napkins, cushion covers and handkerchiefs.

Jewellery. Greece has been renowned since ancient times for its workmanship in gold and silver, and many high-class jewellery stores in Athens still produce superb-quality items, also utilising imported precious stones. Prices are very competitive as gold is sold by weight, with a relatively small mark-up for the crafts-man's skill. Many items incorporate traditional designs that have changed little since ancient times. The major museums also sell copies of popular exhibits.

Although not strictly speaking jewellery, worry beads or *kombologiá* – carried by many older Greek men to calm their nerves – are extremely decorative. The best worry beads feature red coral, black coral, horn, bone or amber, with silver decoration and silk thread. A reputable chain of shops is Kombologadiko (www.kombologadiko.gr).

Icons. These are religious portraits, usually of a saint or sacred event. At the heart of Orthodox worship, they serve as a focus of prayer and a window to the divine.

For centuries icons were popular souvenirs of a grand European tour or religious pilgrimage. However, modern production methods, using thin artificial canvas and gaudy synthetic colours, reduced their popularity. In recent years, however, there has been a rebirth of traditional icon-painting methods, both in church renovations and commercially. Natural pigments and egg tempura binding are painstakingly

Dodgy deals

Prices are fixed everywhere but the flea market, so that's the only place you can really haggle. If you find a deal that is too good to be true for ancient coins, they're probably fakes. Bear in mind that if they're real you're not supposed to take them out of the country anyway. The same applies to all antiquities, with many court cases mounted overseas by the Greek authorities to secure the return of items illegally purchased or otherwise obtained by museums and galleries. Therefore, if you intend to buy an old piece, always use a reputable dealer and obtain an export permit, failing which you will be treated as a smuggler.

mixed and brushed onto a canvas bound over wood. Gold leaf is then applied and the image is given a patina. This time-consuming work is exquisite and expensive.

Pre-1821 icons will require an export permit. You will find mass-produced icons in many tourist shops, but for quality pieces it is worth paying a visit to a specialist store or to the Byzantine Museum's shop.

Edibles and drinks. Non-perishable foodstuffs from the Greek countryside include honey, herbs, olives or olive oil, and pasta like *hilópites* or *trahanás*. For an alcoholic souvenir, try *oúzo* – the aniseed-flavoured national aperitif – or Greek brandy, which is slightly sweeter than French cognac. Metaxa is the main brand; its star rating denotes strength and age.

CHILDREN'S ATHENS

Athens requires some forethought if you are taking young children. Not all will be eager to spend days at the ruins, and summer weather can be oppressively hot. However, children will be welcomed almost everywhere they go.

Eminently child-friendly are the National Gardens (see page 64) with their duck ponds and playground, and the Pédion Áreos, near the National Archaeological Museum, also with play facilities. The Hellenic Children's Museum at Kydathinéon 14 in Pláka (Tue–Fri 10am–2pm, Sat–Sun until 3pm, closed July–Aug; free) has plenty of hands-on activities for youngsters; so too does the permanent interactive 'I play and understand' exhibit opened in 2014 at the Herakleidon Museum (Sun 10am–2pm). Alternatively, a boat trip to a nearby island makes a wonderful day's outing (see page 72), with numerous destinations only one or two hours distant. If all else fails, a day at the beach should blow city cobwebs away (see page 85).

CALENDAR OF EVENTS

1 January: Protohroniá or St Basil's Day, a time of parties and gifts; the traditional greeting is *Kalí Hroniá*.

6 January: Epiphany (Theofánia). Crucifixes are thrown into harbours on all coastlines. The young men who dive and retrieve them receive good luck for the coming year.

February–March: Carnival; masked bands of revellers take to the streets; harmless plastic hammers are sold to hit each other over the head. Tavernas on Tsikhnopémpti (Grill Smell Thursday) are booked out.

Clean Monday (Katharí Deftéra): first day of Lent, 48 days before Easter, marked by kite-flying and outings to the countryside.

25 March: Greek Independence Day/Festival of the Annunciation; military parades.

March/May: Easter (Páskha). The most important Orthodox holiday. Candlelit processions in each parish follow the flower-decked bier of Christ on Good Friday Eve. The resurrection Mass at midnight on Holy Saturday concludes with deafening fireworks and the relaying of the sacred flame from the officiating priests to the parishioners, who carefully take the candles home. On Sunday, lambs are roasted signifying the end of the Lenten fast. *Note that Orthodox Easter does not always fall on the same weekend as Roman Catholic and Protestant Easter.*

1 May: May Day (Protomayiá), marked by flower-gathering excursions to the country – and massive parades by the political Left.

15 August: Dormition of the Virgin (Kímisi tís Panagías). Processions and festivals across the country.

28 October: Óhi Day (*óhi* meaning 'no'), commemorating Greek defiance of the Italian ultimatum of 1940. Patriotic parades.

Mid-November: Athens Marathon commemorates arrival of the news of the defeat of the Persians.

December: Carols are sung door-to-door on the evenings of the twelve days of Christmas. On New Year's Eve, adults play cards for money, and a cake (the *vassilópita*) is baked and served with a coin hidden inside – good luck for whoever gets that slice.

EATING OUT

The backbone of Greek cuisine is local, seasonal ingredients at their peak of flavour, served raw, or cooked simply – on a grill, flash-fried, or slow-baked. Greeks have relied for centuries on staples like olive oil, wild herbs, seafood and lamb or goat's meat, along with an abundance of fresh vegetables, fruit, grains and pulses, washed down with local wine. The traditional Greek diet is one of the healthiest in the world, and prices in all but the flashiest establishments afford excellent value. The prevalence of vegetable and dairy dishes makes eating out a delight for non-meat eaters.

There are numerous places to eat traditional Greek fare across Athens, but, like most other European capitals, it also offers international cuisines as well, in particular Italian and Asian. Greeks love to eat out (large parties should reserve in advance), and new restaurant openings are intently reviewed in the local press. Both Greek and foreign-cuisine restaurants are listed at the end of this chapter (see page 104), but the following information will help you to get the most from any Greek eatery.

Smoking

All restaurant interiors are non-smoking by law. Some surreptitiously provide ash-trays on demand, however if you wish to smoke overtly, usually this must be done outside.

WHERE TO EAT

You will find a range of Greek eating establishments, each type specialising in certain dishes, and many still family-run. The *psistaría* offers charcoal-grilled meats, plus a limited selection of salads and *mezédes*. The *tavérna* is a more elaborate eatery,

Café Thission, in the neighbourhood of the same name

offering the pre-cooked, steam-tray dishes known as *magireftá*, as well as a few grills and bulk wine. Restaurants (*estiatória*) and *inomagiría* (wine-and-food canteens) overlap considerably with tavernas, though are less likely to have grilled items. The *ouzerí* purveys not just *oúzo*, but also the *mezédes* dishes that complement it – *oúzo* is never drunk on an empty stomach. Octopus, olives, a bit of cheese or a platter of small fried fish are traditional accompaniments, but there are various other hot and cold vegetable or meat dishes to choose from. For sticky cakes, retire to a *zaharoplastío* – pastry or sweet shop – or a *galaktopolío*, which emphasises yoghurt, puddings and other milk-based dishes.

The *kafenío* is the Greek coffee shop, traditionally a men-only domain, and still so in the countryside. Usually very plainly decorated (though tables and chairs are smarter of late), it is the venue for political debate and serious backgammon (and card) games. Only drinks – both alcoholic and soft – are served.

Meal times

Lunch is eaten between 2.30 and 4pm. Traditionally this meal would be followed by a siesta before work began again at 5.30pm, but this custom is on the wane in Athens. Dinner is usually eaten from 9.30pm, with many establishments taking last orders as late as 1am. If you want to eat early, some tavernas begin service at around 7pm, but most don't even open until 8pm. You will have your choice of table then, but the atmosphere is definitely better later. Sunday evening and part of or all of Monday are typical times of closure for those tavernas which do not operate daily.

WHAT TO EAT

You will usually be given an extensive menu (often in both Greek and English); items currently available will have a price pencilled in beside them. However, your waiter is a more reliable guide to what is available each day; the menu is most useful for checking that the taverna is within your budget – especially for typically pricey items like meat or fish. It is also the rule to inspect the steam trays or chiller case to see what looks and smells enticing; this is a good way to familiarise yourself with the various Greek dishes.

All restaurants have a cover charge. This includes a serving of bread and usually costs no more than €1–1.50 per person.

Appetisers

Carefully selected appetisers (*mezédes*) can constitute a full meal. Shared by the whole table, they are a fun and relaxing way to eat – you have as little or as much as you want and keep ordering until you have had your fill. *Ouzerís* in particular have no qualms about taking orders for 'mezédes only' meals, bringing your choices out on a *dískos* or tray – though there is an optional second round of hot mains, made-to-order.

Tzatzíki, crispy fried aubergine and gígandes

The most common appetisers are *tzatzíki*, a yoghurt dip flavoured with garlic, cucumber and mint; *dolmádes*, vine leaves stuffed with rice and vegetables – rarely mince – which can be served hot (with egg-lemon sauce) or cold (with yoghurt); olives; *taramosaláta*, cod-roe paste blended with breadcrumbs, olive oil and lemon juice; *skordaliá*, garlic-and-potato sauce served with fried vegetable slices; *gígandes*, large beans in tomato sauce; *kalamarákia*, deep-fried small squid; *mavromátika*, black-eyed peas; *tyrokapterí*, a spicy cheese dip; and *hórta*, boiled wild greens. *Saganáki* is hard cheese coated in breadcrumbs and then fried, while *féta psití* is feta cheese wrapped in foil with garlic and herbs – often spicy ones – and baked.

Greek salad or *horiátiki saláta* (usually translated as 'village salad') consists of tomato, cucumber, onion, green peppers and olives topped with feta cheese. Cruets of olive oil and wine vinegar are found with other condiments on the table.

Fish

Athens' proximity to the sea means that fresh fish (*psári*) is readily available, and throughout Attica you will find excellent seafood restaurants (*psarotavérnes*). The day's catch is displayed on ice inside a chiller case for you to make your choice, which will be weighed, uncleaned, before cooking – check prices first as seafood is always a relatively expensive option. If the seafood is frozen or farmed (very likely from June to September), this must by law be stated on the menu – though often only in the Greek-language column, or simply with an asterisk.

Larger fish is usually grilled and smaller fish fried; all are served with fresh lemon and *ladolémono* (olive oil with lemon juice). Most common species are *barboúni* (red mullet), *xifías* (swordfish), *tsipoúra* (gilt-head bream) and *fangrí* (bream). *Marídes* (picarel), *gávros* (anchovy) and *sardélles* (sardines) are served crisp-fried. More elaborate seafood dishes include *okhtapódi krasáto*, octopus in red wine and tomato sauce; *soupiá* (cuttlefish) with spinach-rice; or *garídes* (prawns) in a cheese sauce (*saganáki*). Fish soup, *psarósoupa*, is most common during the cooler months.

Taverna fruit platters

Complimentary platters of fruit (*froúto*) typically feature watermelon or Persian melon in summer; grapes or pears in autumn; sliced apples with cinnamon much of the year; and citrus fruit or strawberries in early spring. Greece imports just a few temperate fruits from Italy or Spain, and relatively little tropical fruit, so this is pretty much the repertoire.

Meat and casserole dishes

Meaty take-away snacks include *gýros* (thin slices of fatty pork cut from a vertical skewer and served with tomatoes, *tzatzíki* and lettuce in pitta bread), or *souvláki* (small chunks of meat cooked on a skewer). Sit-down barbecued dishes include whole chickens, sides of lamb or *kondosoúvli* (rotisseried pork), all cooked to a melting perfection. If you want a basic pork or veal cutlet, ask for *brizóla*; lamb or goat chops, however, are *païdákia*.

Fresh seafood platter

Greece's most famous slow-cooked oven dish is probably *moussakás* – successive layers of potatoes, aubergine and minced beef topped with a generous layer of béchamel sauce. It should be firm but succulent, and aromatic with nutmeg; good restaurants make a fresh batch daily. *Pastítsio* is another layered dish of macaroni, meat and cheese sauce. Other common casseroles include *giouvétsi* (any meat baked in a clay pot with lozenge-shaped *kritharáki* pasta) and *kokinistó* or *stifádo*, braised meat – especially rabbit – with baby onions.

For a hot meatless dish, *gemistá* are tomatoes or peppers stuffed with herb-flavoured rice (though meat stock may be used); alternatively, *melitzánes imám* (aubergine stuffed richly with tomato, onions and oil) is reliably vegetarian, as is *briám* or *tourloú* (ratatouille).

Cheeses

Greek cheeses are made from cow's, ewe's or goat's milk, or blends of two milks in varying proportions. The best-known cheese is *féta*, popping up in every Greek salad or served alone garnished with olive oil and oregano. *Graviéra* is the most common hard cheese, varying in sharpness; there are also many sweet soft cheeses such as *myzíthra*, *manoúri* and *anthótyro*.

Dessert

Most tavernas bring a plate of seasonal fresh fruit or semolina halva as a finale to your meal; for something more substantial, the *zaharoplastío* (sticky-cake shop) dishes out some of the more enduring legacies of the Ottomans, who introduced incredibly decadent sweets: *baklavás*, layers of honey-soaked flaky pastry with walnuts; *kataïfi*, 'shredded wheat' filled with chopped almonds

⊙ BULK WINE AND RETSÍNA

Most tavernas offer house wine in bulk – ask for *krasí hýma* or *varelísio* – which is usually cheaper than bottled varieties. It comes in full, half or quarter-litre measures, served either in coloured aluminium cups called *katroútza*, or in glass flagons. This basic, rustic wine – whether red, white or rosé – will be served young and cool (cold in the case of white). Quality varies considerably; if in doubt, order a quarter-litre to start with, and/or a can of soda to dilute it. Bulk wine is either *aretsínato* (unresined) or *retsína* (flavoured with pine resin). *Retsína* has been around since ancient times, when Greeks accidentally discovered the preservative properties of treating wine with pine resin. It complements the olive-oil base of oven-cooked dishes perfectly, but can be an acquired taste and should be served well chilled. The best bulk *retsína* traditionally came from Attica's Mesógeia district, but nowadays there are good bottled brands like Malamatina, Georgiadi and Liokri.

Enjoying an ouzo with lunch at Athens' central market

and honey; *galaktoboúreko*, custard pie; or *ravaní*, honey-soaked sponge cake. If you prefer dairy desserts, try yoghurt topped with local honey; *kréma* (custard), or *ryzógalo*, cold rice pudding.

WHAT TO DRINK

Anise-flavoured *oúzo* is taken as an aperitif with ice and water; a compound in the anise flavouring makes the mix turn harmlessly cloudy. The most popular brands (like Mini and Plomari) come from the island of Lésvos. *Tsípouro* is a north-mainland variant of this grape-mash distillate, usually without anise. Another similar distilled spirit is *tsikoudiá* which originates from Crete, though most Cretans refer to it by its Turkish name, *rakí*.

There are nearly a dozen brands of beer produced in Greece, as well as imports. Foreign brands made under licence include Amstel, Kaiser and Heineken; local labels are Fix (reckoned the best), Alfa, Mythos, Pils Hellas and Vergina.

For a digestif, Metaxa is the most popular domestic brandy, sold (in ascending order of strength and aging) in 3-, 5- and 7-star grades.

Non-alcoholic drinks

Hot coffee (*kafés*) is served *ellínikós*, 'Greek' style (generic Middle Eastern style), freshly brewed in copper pots and served in small cups. It will automatically arrive *glykós* (very sweet) unless you order *métrios* (medium) or *skétos* (without sugar). Don't drink to the bottom as that's where the grounds settle! Instant coffee (called 'Nes' irrespective of brand) has made big inroads in Greece; more appetising is *frappés*, cold instant whipped up in a blender with sugar and milk *(gála)*, especially refreshing on a summer's day. Most cafés and bars serve Italian-style espresso and cappuccino – though expect to pay Italian prices – and for fans of milky Seattle coffee, Starbucks can be found in Athens at various locations.

Soft drinks come in all the international varieties, while juices are most likely out of cardboard cartons. Bottled (*enfialoméno*) still mineral water is typically from Crete or the Greek mainland mountains. Souroti and Epsa are the most widespread domestic sparkling brands. Soda water is usually Tuborg.

TO HELP YOU ORDER

Could we have a table? **Boroúme na éhoume éna trapézi?**
May we order, please? **Na parangiloúme, parakaló?**
A litre/a half litre **Éna kiló/misó kilo**
I'm a vegetarian **Íme hortofágos**
The bill, please **To logariazmó, parakaló**

plate **piáto**	glass **potíri**
napkin **hartopetséta**	bread **psomí**
cutlery **maheropírouna**	butter **voútyro**

sugar **záhari**
salt **aláti**
pepper **pipéri**
oil **ládi**

MENU READER

fried **tiganitó**
baked **sto foúrno**
roasted **psitó**
grilled **sta kárvouna**
stuffed **gemistá**
fish **psári**
small shrimp **garídes**
octopus **okhtapódi**
red mullet **barboúni**
swordfish **xifías**
meat **kréas**
meatballs **keftedákia**
beef **moskhári**
pork **hirinó**
chicken **kotópoulo**
goat **katsíki**
lamb **arní**
rabbit **kounélli**
salad **saláta**
tomatoes **domátes**

Traditional Greek coffee

olives **eliés**
boiled greens **hórta**
runner beans **fasolákia**
aubergine/eggplants
   melitzána
chickpeas **revýthia**
cheese **tyrí**
wine **krasí**
beer **býra**
water **neró**

USEFUL EXPRESSIONS

Kalí órexi Bon appétit
Kalí synnéhia Enjoy the rest of your meal (literally 'Good
   continuation')
Yiámas Cheers (as a toast)

PLACES TO EAT

Most of the following recommendations are central and/or close to public transport routes. Prices indicated are for dinner per person with modest intake of wine, beer or tsípouro.

€€€€€	over 40 euros
€€€€	30–40 euros
€€€	22–30 euros
€€	15–22 euros
€	under 15 euros

EXÁRHIA

Atitamos € *Kapodistríou 2, metro Omónia, tel: 210 33 00 864.* This small and friendly restaurant offers a short but well-selected menu of traditional Greek fare. Try the lamb in lemon sauce or the succulent octopus. Booking is recommended, especially on weekends when it gets packed. Open daily breakfast, lunch and dinner. Cash only.

Avli € *Methónis 43, tel: 210 38 38 167.* There is a small avlí (courtyard) here, but most seating is inside this engaging old-house taverna doing all the standard oven dishes and appetizers (plus some creative recipes like chicken-and-spinach soufflé) with a deft touch. Open Mon–Sat lunch and dinner, closed Sun and Aug. Cash only.

Pinaleon €€ *Mavromiháli 152, metro Ambelókipi, tel: 210 64 40 945.* This indoor taverna enjoys a cult following for its rich *mezédes* (offered on a *dískos*), mains such as smoked pork loin in *mastic* sauce and own-brewed red wine. It is usually lively, with close-packed tables, so best to book, especially Wednesdays when there's live music. Open late Sept–mid-May, dinner only. Cash only.

Rakoumel €–€€ *Emmanouíl Benáki 71, metro Omónia, tel: 210 38 00 506.* A favourite among several Cretan-cuisine spots in Athens, with delicacies like fennel pie, Sfakian sausages and seasonal greens imported from Crete; and of course, *paximádia* (rusks) instead of bread, and Cretan *rakí* by the carafe. Seating on the sidewalk or inside. Open daily lunch and dinner. Cash only.

Rosebud €€ *Omírou 40, metro Panepistímio, tel: 210 33 92 370, www.rosebud. gr.* Creative vegan and vegetarian food served in a casual, modern setting, often to the backdrop of live jazz. Delicious vegetable *moussakás*, *gýros* and pizza. There is also a colourful bar. Open daily breakfast, lunch and dinner.

Rozalia €€ *Valtetsíou 54, metro Omónia, tel: 210 3302 933, www.rozalia.gr.* Located on a pretty pedestrianised street, this spacious taverna is well known for its excellent *mezédes* and wide selection of authentic Greek fare. Mouth-watering vegetarian options. Open daily lunch and dinner.

KOLONÁKI

Filippou €€ *Xenokrátous 19, metro Evangelismós, tel: 210 72 16 390.* Since 1923, this estiatório has served honest fare such as *angináres* (artichokes) *à la políta* and rabbit, washed down with excellent bulk wine. Service is low-key but efficient; the dining room has a pleasant retro air with proper table napery and terracotta flooring, plus there's a small outdoor terrace. Open daily lunch and dinner, except Sat eve, Sun and part of Aug. Cash only.

Oikeio €€ *Ploutárchou 15, metro Evangelismós, tel: 210 72 59 216.* In this boutique-style restaurant the chef prepares tasty, reasonably-priced Mediterranean dishes with a modern twist. The sea bass with lemon is really worth a try. Open daily lunch and dinner.

Il Postino €€ *Grivéon 3, pedestrian lane off Skoufá, metro Panepistimíou, tel: 210 36 41 414.* A genuine *osteria* with an unpretentious menu, supervised by an Italian chef with an illustrious track record in Athens. Sit in the quiet cul-de-sac outside or inside with its old-photo décor and retro music. Open daily lunch and dinner.

MAKRYGIÁNNI/PLÁKA

Edodi €€€€ *Veïkoú 80, metro Syngroú-Fix, tel: 210 92 13 013, www.edodi. gr.* One of Athens' best 'nouvelle' restaurants, an intimate, eight-table affair run attentively by two brothers on the upper floor of a neoclassical house. The international fusion menu changes regularly but is likely to include dishes such as duck in cherry sauce or smoked-goose carpaccio. Save room for the creative desserts. Open Mon–Sat, dinner only; closed summer.

Furin Kazan €€€–€€€€ *Apóllonos 2, metro Sýndagma, tel: 210 32 29 170,* www.furin-kazan.com. Considered the best surviving Japanese eatery in Athens – and knots of Japanese tourists seem to think so too, making booking advisable. Mostly sushi on offer, as well as token tempura dishes and appetizers. Despite reasonable portion sizes, it's no bargain – but Japanese food is always overpriced in Greece. Open daily lunch and dinner.

Kapnikarea €€ *Hristopoúlou 2, corner Ermoú, metro Monastiráki, tel: 210 32 27 394.* The food at this *ouzerí* – sausages, *saganáki*, aubergine dishes, good salads – is only slightly bumped up in price thanks to the acoustic *rebétika* musicians who play here every afternoon. Seating is outdoors in this pedestrianised lane, with awnings and heaters for winter. Daily lunch only, may open Fri/Sat eves too, closed summer.

Mani-Mani €€€–€€€€ *Falírou 10, metro Acropolis, tel: 210 92 18 180,* www.manimani.com.gr. Installed in the top floor of a graceful interwar house, this established nouvelle-Greek-cuisine restaurant does (as the name implies) have a marked Peloponnesian tendency, what with *sýnglino* (streaky pork) and *talagáni* cheese from Messinía on the menu; but there's a wide variety of *mezédes*, salads, pasta dishes and even some seafood, as well as creative desserts. Open Tue–Sat lunch and dinner, Sun lunch only.

Platanos €€–€€€ *Diogénous 4, metro Monastiráki, tel: 210 32 20 666.* With tables on a square shaded by a *plátanos* (plane tree) near the Tower of the Winds, this 1932-founded taverna focuses on stews – lamb-based are best – and *laderá* (vegetable casseroles), though portions could be bigger. The barrelled *retsína* has been featured in wine guides as an example of what it should be. Closed Sun night and Aug. Cash only.

MONASTIRÁKI/PSYRRÍ/THISSÍO

Café Avissinia €€€ *Kynéttou 7, metro Monastiráki, tel: 210 32 17 047.* After browsing the weekend flea market, this is an atmospheric place to retire for hearty, Middle-Eastern-influenced food and a spot of entertainment courtesy of strolling accordionists and singers. Upstairs and outdoor tables are quieter. Open Tue–Sat lunch and dinner, Sun lunch only, closed summer.

Nikitas € *Agíon Anargýron 19, metro Monastiráki, tel 210 32 52 591.* Probably the oldest (1967-founded) taverna in Psyrrí, Nikítas purveys a short but sweet menu, as well as daily specials like oven-baked cheese pie. Drink is confined to beer or *óuzo*, and there are no sweets. But for good value you can't beat it, especially if seated outdoors under the trees beside Agíon Anargýron church. Open Mon–Sat lunch. Cash only.

Steki tou Ilia €€ *Eptahálkou 5, tel 210 34 58 052,* and *Thessaloníkis 7, tel 210 34 22 407, metro Thissío.* The two branches (open alternately) of this enterprise fill with locals here for the house speciality: a big platter of grilled succulent lamb chops. Starters like *fáva*, *tzatzíki* and *hórta* are more than competent, service is quick, and barrelled wine is reasonable. Take a table outside, or sit indoors under the wine barrels. Open Tue–Sat dinner only, Sun lunch, closed Mon. Cash only.

Taverna tou Psyrri €€ *Eskhlýlou 12, metro Monastiráki, tel: 210 32 14 923.* Trendy, expensive eateries are ten a penny in Psyrrí; this is one of the few normally priced traditional tavernas, and accordingly popular, so show up early. The menu is strong on fish and seafood, as well as the usual suspects mezés-wise. There is a garden out back, and the inside is decorated with old photos and gravures of Athens. Open daily lunch and dinner. Cash only.

Thanassis € *Mitropóleos 69, tel: 210 32 44 705,* http://othanasis.com. Three hotly competing *souvlatzídika* (souvlaki stalls) cluster here just before Platía Monastirakioú, but the queues make it obvious which is the best. Thanassis' speciality is Middle Eastern kebab, mincemeat blended with onion and spices. The side dish of chili peppers will blow your head off. Open daily breakfast, lunch and dinner. Cash only.

OMÓNIA

Athinaïkon €€ *Themistokléos 2, metro Omónia, tel: 210 38 38 485,* www.athinaikon.gr. This *ouzerí,* founded in 1932 but installed here since 1987, is famous for its seafood *mezédes* like mussels *saganáki,* paella and cockles; meat platters are less distinguished. Much of the attraction lies in classy décor, with antique trim and marble tables, and efficient service. Busy at lunch with local business people. Open Mon–Sat lunch and dinner, closed Aug.

Diporto €€ *Sokrátous 9, corner Theátrou 2, metro Omónia, tel: 210 32 11 463.* Diporto ('double entrance') is a completely unsignposted basement *inomagerío* tucked under derelict commercial premises. A diverse clientele, from 'suits' to nearby market-stall holders, flock here for the no-nonsense nosh: spicy beef on *kritharáki* pasta, chickpeas, little fishes. Bulk *retsína* is served on a block of ice in warm weather; the marble sink for glass-washing and filling the *retsína* tins is a work of art. Just 24 covers, so diners are expected to share the 6 tables with strangers. Open Mon–Sat lunch and dinner. Cash only.

Klimataria €€ *Platía Theátrou 2, metro Omónia, tel: 210 32 16 629.* An excellent source of hearty cooking with dishes such as stir-fry with leeks or mature lamb with *stamnagáthi* greens – the row of *gástres,* the traditional backcountry stew pots, tip you off as you enter. There are vegetarian and fish choices (such as stewed vegetables and stuffed *thrápsalo*) too, and top-notch live acoustic music on Fri–Sat eve and Sun lunch (booking mandatory). Open daily lunch and dinner. Cash only.

PANGRÁTI

Colibri €€ *Empedokléous 9–13, no metro, tel: 210 70 11 011.* After taking in the National Gallery or the Byzantine and Christian Museum, it's worth walking to lunch at this superior pizza, burger and pasta outfit, the most tourist-convenient of a local three-outlet chain. Salads are scrumptious, thin-crust pizzas excellent value in two sizes, and red bulk wine a bargain. The owner once ran a restaurant in Sweden, and the kitchen is scrubbed top to bottom nightly – so no rancid-oil smells here.

Outdoor tables on the pedestrian street are much sought-after in summer. Open daily lunch and dinner. Cash only.

Karavitis €€–€€€ *Arktínou 33 and Pafsaníou 4, metro Evangelismós, tel: 210 72 15 155*. Pangráti's last surviving 1930s taverna, relying on baked casseroles, a few *mezédes* or grills, and *Mesógia* bulk wine. Traditional desserts like quince or semolina halva; outdoor seating in a lovely garden across the street, indoors houses the now-empty wine barrels. Open daily dinner, Sun also lunch. Cash only.

Katsourbos €€€ *Aminda 2, tel: 210 72 22 167*, www.katsourbos.gr. A cosy restaurant specialising in Cretan cuisine. Fried cheese with honey, *dolmadakia* and lamb chops are firm favourites. Open daily lunch and dinner.

Spondi €€€€€ *Pýrronos 5, tel: 210 75 20 658*, www.spondi.gr. With the kitchen under the command of a French chef, and seating in a neoclassical house and its courtyard, Michelin-starred Spondi is ideal for special occasions (or those with expense accounts – count on €170 per person). Creative, often improbable, fusion cuisine combines assorted influences in herb- or truffle-flavoured duck, meat and fish dishes followed by decadent dessert concoctions. Closed lunch and Aug.

Vyrinis €€ *Arhimídous 11, tel: 210 7012153*. Much-loved local taverna, now being managed by the Anglo-Greek grandsons of the founder. They've made decor more contemporary with butcher-paper table coverings and a large, swooping awning in the summer courtyard, but the old mosaic floor and wine barrels have stayed – as has the good-value fare, mainly salads, starters and creative mains. Almost uniquely hereabouts, open at lunch as well as dinner (not Sun eve).

PETRÁLONA

Askimopapo € *Ionón 61; metro Petrálona; tel 210 34 63 282*. Founded in 1968 by leftist actor Andonis Voulgaris, the bohemian 'Ugly Duckling' is now run alternate days by his daughters. The inside is lined with old theatre photos and pen-and-ink or charcoal sketches donated by admirers (many foreign). The food – a mix of meat-based *magireftá* and vegetarian starters – is plainly presented but well-priced and wholesome; Límnos white wine or Neméa red to drink. Open Oct 1 to mid-June Mon–Sat dinner only; cash only.

Oikonomou €€ *Tröon 41, corner Kydantidón, metro Petrálona, tel: 210 34 67 555.* Crowded pavement tables rather than the sign over the door announce you've come to this *inomagerío* which does just a handful of dishes per day: *laderá*, cabbage *dolmádes*, roast meat, a limited repertoire of starters in big portions. There's red wine or good *retsína* from the barrel. Inside, enjoy the old coloured engravings of Attica and caricatures of wine-drinkers. Open Mon–Sat dinner only; cash only.

Santorinios € *Doriéon 8, metro Petrálona, tel: 210 34 51 629.* Cult taverna installed in an old refugee compound and barrel-making workshop from 1926; seating is in small rooms or the lovely courtyard. If some dishes and frequently distracted service rate only three-and-a-half stars, the atmosphere and low prices merit four to five. Open Sept–June Mon–Sat dinner only, July–Aug Sun lunch only. Cash only.

BEYOND ATHENS

Albatros € *Konstandínou Sathá 36, Galaxídi, tel: 22650 42233.* Very congenial taverna run by an older couple, whose limited daily offerings might include rabbit stew, *gemistá*, octopus in wine, baked pies or the house speciality *samári* (pancetta in sauce). Tables indoors, or outside under trees strung with fairy lights. Open daily lunch and dinner. Cash only.

Geitoniko (Manolis & Khristina's) €€ *inland lane beyond Bratsera Hotel and Xeri Elia Taverna, Ýdra (Hydra), tel: 22980 53615.* Perhaps the best all-rounder on the island, doing *magireftá*, fish, grills and starters equally well; seating either downstairs or up on the roof terrace. Open daily March–Nov lunch and dinner. Cash only.

Patralis €€€–€€€€ *Kounoupítsa district, Spétses, tel: 22980 75380.* Upmarket and delightfully old fashioned, this has long ranked as the best – and best-value – seafood taverna on the island. Well-priced wine list, complimentary dessert and careful service round off the experience. Open daily lunch and dinner.

A–Z TRAVEL TIPS

A SUMMARY OF PRACTICAL INFORMATION

A Accommodation _____ 112
Airport _____ 112
B Budgeting for
your trip _____ 113
C Car hire _____ 113
Climate _____ 115
Clothing _____ 115
Complaints _____ 116
Crime and safety _____ 116
D Driving _____ 117
E Electricity _____ 119
Embassies and
consulates _____ 119
Emergencies _____ 120
G Gay and lesbian
travellers _____ 120
Getting there _____ 120
Guides and tours _____ 121
H Health and medical
care _____ 122

L Language _____ 123
M Maps _____ 125
Media _____ 125
Money _____ 125
O Opening times _____ 126
P Police _____ 126
Post offices _____ 127
Public
holidays _____ 127
T Telephones _____ 128
Time zones _____ 128
Tipping _____ 128
Toilets _____ 128
Tourist
information _____ 129
Transport _____ 129
V Visas and entry
requirements _____ 131
W Websites _____ 131
Y Youth hostels _____ 131

A

ACCOMMODATION

Hotels. Since a pre-Olympic Games overhaul of most Athens hotels, very little remains here that could be called budget accommodation, at least of the savoury variety – count on paying at least €70 for a double room, which figure should include municipal tax and VAT. Most hotels appear on generic hotel-booking websites, or have their own site.

Prices fluctuate across the year, with a difference of as much as 50 percent between high and low seasons. Savvy travellers have learned that Athens is at its most pleasant in May–June and September–October, and these are now reckoned peak seasons by most hoteliers; it can be easier to secure a vacancy during July and August, but you should book well ahead year-round to avoid disappointment. Reservations of less than three nights may attract a surcharge.

> I'd like a single/double room **Tha íthela éna monóklino/ díklino**
> How much do you charge? **Póso hreónete?**

AIRPORT

The **Eleftheríos Venizélos airport** serving Athens is 27km (18 miles) from Sýndagma Square in the heart of the city. The airport **express bus** X95 (24 hours) will take you directly to Sýndagma Square in just over an hour if traffic is light (almost two hours in heavy traffic); departures are every quarter-hour during the day, half-hourly between 11pm and 6am. At peak traffic times, and with light luggage, consider alighting at the Ethnikí Ámyna or Nomismatokopío metro stations and continuing your journey into town from there, but this works out slightly more expensive (if quicker) than using the infrequent (half-hourly) **metro** all the way from the airport station. If you're headed out straight to the islands, or a beach suburb, it makes most sense to use the X96 express bus, which links the airport up to three times hourly with Karaïskáki Square in Piraeus via Vári, Voúla and Glyfáda.

The fare for all express buses is €6 and the ticket is only valid for a single journey into town, without using the metro. Buy your ticket at the kiosk outside the arrivals hall and validate it on the machine as you board the bus. The metro ticket costs €10 for a single traveller, €18 for two persons, €24 for three.

A **taxi** will take about the same time as the X95 bus and should cost €35–40 from the airport to Sýndagma Square.

B

BUDGETING FOR YOUR TRIP

These are some rough estimates for your main expenses:
Scheduled return flight from London: £120–£300 depending on season.
Scheduled flight from New York: $500–$1300 depending on season.
Hotel room in mid-range hotel in high season: €70–160 per night.
Meal in mid-range taverna with house wine (per person): €20–25.
Weekly car rental for a small car in high season: €260 unlimited mileage with a small local chain, €350 with a major international chain. In low season this range becomes €150–€250. Especially if you want to pick up your car at the airport, it's worth pre-booking a car online before your journey.
One-way hydrofoil/catamaran ticket to Égina: €14; to Póros: €14; to Ýdra: €28 (cheaper by ferry).

C

CAR HIRE (see also Driving)

Athens is a very congested city with a critical (and expensive) parking situation; the main tourist attractions are concentrated in such a small area that it makes little sense to hire a car. Using public transport will limit the amount of walking you do, and taxis are plentiful and affordable. However, if you intend to spend a few days touring the Argolid or heading for Delphi, a car would definitely be an asset.

Those intending to hire a car should carry an International Driving Permit if from the US, Canada or Australia (national licences alone are not valid, and there are heavy fines if you're detected driving without an IDP). Alternatively, all European Economic Area national driver's licences are accepted, provided that they have been held for one full year and the driver is over 21 years of age (sometimes 23 years for certain agencies). You will also need a credit or debit card for a deposit.

Many brochure rates seem attractive because they do not include personal insurance, collision damage waiver (CDW) or VAT at 23 percent. Most agencies have a waiver excess of between €400 and €600 – the amount you're responsible for if your vehicle gets smashed or stolen, even with CDW coverage. It is strongly suggested you purchase extra cover (often called Super CDW or Liability Waiver Surcharge) to reduce this risk to zero; UK or North American residents can buy good-value annual policies from companies like Insurance4CarHire (www.insurance4carhire.com).

All the major international chains are represented in the arrivals concourse of the airport. In central Athens, almost all rental companies have offices at the start of Syngroú Avenue in Makrigiánni district, and comparison shopping for quotes a day or so before you need a car can be very productive. Some smaller but reputable agencies to try include:

Autorent, Syngroú 9, tel: 210 92 20 821, www.autorent.gr
Avance, Syngroú 40–42, tel: 210 92 00 100, www.avance.gr
Avanti, Syngroú 50, tel: 210 92 33 919, www.avanti.com.gr
Budget, Syngroú 23, tel: 210 92 14 771, www.budget.com
Kosmos, Syngroú 9, tel: 210 92 34 695, www.kosmos-carrental.com

I'd like to rent a car (tomorrow) for three days/a week **Tha íthela na nikiáso éna avtokínito (ávrio) giá tris méres/ mía evdomáda**

CLIMATE

Athens has a surprising range of climatic conditions and temperatures. Most summer days feature dry, furnace-like heat. Many Athenians leave the city during this season, and if you can avoid it, don't visit between late June and mid-September. From early June until the end of September, the weather is hot during the day and warm in the evenings, with 12–15 hours of sunshine per day. Between early October and late April, the weather can be quite changeable, with occasional wet and windy days. Snow occasionally falls in winter, but rain is more common.

Average air temperatures:

		J	F	M	A	M	J	J	A	S	O	N	D
Max	°C	12	12	16	19	25	32	44	38	29	23	20	15
Max	°F	54	54	60	66	76	90	110	100	85	74	65	58
Min	°C	2	7	8	11	16	19	23	23	19	16	11	8
Min	°F	35	44	46	52	60	66	72	72	66	60	52	46

Average water temperatures (Piraeus):

	J	F	M	A	M	J	J	A	S	O	N	D
°C	14	14	13	15	18	22	25	25	24	22	18	16
°F	57	57	55	59	64	72	77	77	75	72	64	61

CLOTHING

From early June to late September, light, natural-fibre summer clothing should suffice – with perhaps a wrap for later in the evening. Even though you are in a city, take anti-sunburn precautions; hats, sunglasses and long, loose sleeves are a must in summer.

In spring and autumn, bring extra layers in case of a cold spell. In winter, bring a heavy coat or waterproof jacket, and a pocket umbrella, as Athens can be cold and wet. There are often pleasant days late or early in the year, so a layering system – i.e. a pullover/sweater plus a light shell jacket – as for spring or autumn works well.

If you intend to enter any of the churches in the city you must be suitably dressed. No shorts for either sex, and women must have shoulders covered. Shorts on men are considered infra dig at any season – you'll see Athenians sweltering away in woollen slacks even in summer.

Comfortable, practical footwear is essential for touring archaeological sites. Marble steps and walkways are worn slippery with age; other surfaces are uneven, which can result in twisted ankles.

COMPLAINTS (see also Police)

If you have a complaint, first take it up with the management of the establishment concerned. If, however, you get no satisfaction then you can approach the Tourist Police (tel: 171; offices on Dimitrakopoúlou near corner Anastasíou Zínni, Koukáki district) whose English-speaking officers are specifically trained to deal with visitor problems – anything from petty theft to lost passports and complaints about taxi drivers, shopkeepers, tour guides and the like.

CRIME AND SAFETY

Central Athens is generally safer than most north-European or American cities, but the ongoing economic crisis and laxly controlled immigration has meant that crimes against people and property have shown a sharp rise recently.

Organised gangs of pickpockets target new arrivals stepping off the airport bus at Sýndagma, and are also particularly active in Monastiráki station. You know it's about to happen when several of them corral you in a metro car (new or old lines) and then press you against the wall, the better to relieve you of your pocket contents – at which they are very skilled.

If the worst happens, contact credit-card issuers immediately – your cards will be used to obtain fraudulent cash advances within minutes at Sýndagma bureaux de change. You will, of course, have also stashed away a photocopy of your passport, as well as records of your card numbers (and the theft-reporting hotline) in a secure section of your luggage. Sadly, the police are unlikely to do anything on your behalf other than issue a report for you to use when making insurance claims.

Once settled in your hotel, leave valuables and cash surplus to daily requirements in the room safe. Leave nothing of value visible in parked cars, especially in Psyrrí and Exárhia where break-ins are rife.

Sýndagma is also the focus of regular rallies against austerity measures. They can deteriorate into confrontations between police and demonstrators, but 'events' are well publicised and it's simple enough to stay well clear on the day.

D

DRIVING

Road conditions. Athens' streets are often gridlocked, so on many occasions you can make better progress walking than driving. Drivers jostle for position, often running a changing (if not red) light, and park wherever they please. Keep on the alert whether you are driving or walking.

The centre of Athens, the so-called *daktýlios*, has alternate-day driving midweek. That is, vehicles with odd-numbered licence plates may enter the central zone on odd-numbered days, and even-numbered cars on even days – Monday to Thursday 7am to 8pm, Friday 7am to 3pm, from early September to mid-July. There are, however, numerous exemptions, including rental cars.

Most roads in the countryside have no verges or hard shoulders. This can cause problems if you need to leave the highway. If you get caught in a storm the road surface can become treacherously slippery, especially in May when oily olive-tree blossom is dropping; most roads being banked wrongly at curves aggravates this problem.

Rules and regulations. Traffic drives on the right and passes on the left, usually yielding to vehicles from the right (from the left on roundabouts) – though this is not always observed, and accident rates are high.

> Fill the tank, please. **Óso pérnei, parakaló.**
> My car has broken down **To avtokínito mou éhi halási**
> There's been an accident **Ehi gínei dystíhima**

The speed limit on motorways is 120kmh (74mph), 90kmh (55mph) on undivided roads, and in built-up areas 50kmh (30mph) unless otherwise stated, although these are widely disregarded. Both speed limit and distance signs are in kilometres.

Road signs. Most road signs are the standard pictographs used across Europe. However, you may also meet some of these written signs:

> **ΑΠΑΓΟΡΕΥΕΤΑΙ Η ΑΝΑΜΟΝΗ** No waiting
> **ΑΠΑΓΟΡΕΥΕΤΑΙ Η ΕΙΣΟΔΟΣ** No entry
> **ΑΠΑΓΟΡΕΥΕΤΑΙ Η ΣΤΑΘΜΕΥΣΙΣ** No parking
> **ΔΙΑΒΑΣΙΣΠΕΖΩΝ** Pedestrian crossing
> **ΕΛΤΤΩΣΑΤΕ ΤΑΧΥΤΗΤΑ** Reduce speed
> **ΕΡΓΑ ΕΠΙ ΤΗΣ ΟΔΟΥ** Road work in progress
> **ΚΙΝΔΥΝΟΣ** Caution
> **ΜΟΝΟΔΡΟΜΟΣ** One-way traffic
> **ΠΑΡΑΚΑΜΠΤΗΡΙΟΣ** Diversion (detour)
> **ΑΛΤ/ΣΤΟΠ** Stop

If you need help. If you have an accident or breakdown while on the road, put a red warning triangle some distance behind you to warn oncoming traffic. Always carry the telephone number of your rental office; they will advise you in case of difficulty. If you have an accident involving another vehicle, or injury to persons or stationary property, do not admit fault or move either car until the traffic police *(trohéa)* come out and prepare a report; a copy will be given to you to present to the rental agency. Almost all agencies subscribe to one of the nationwide emergency roadside services (ELPA, Express Service, Ellas Service, Intersalonica); make sure you are given the pertinent number.

E

ELECTRICITY

The electric current throughout Greece is 220 volts/50 cycles. Electric plugs are of the European continental double round-pin type. North-American-to-continental (but not UK-to-continental) adapter plugs are available from electrical shops. Don't bring strictly 120-volt equipment – most modern hairdryers and shavers should have a dual voltage setting.

a transformer **énas metaskhimatistís**
an adapter **énas prosarmostís**

EMBASSIES AND CONSULATES

Australian Embassy and Consulate Level 6, Thon Building, junction Kifisías & Alexándras, 115 21 Athens; tel: 210 87 04 000, www.greece. embassy.gov.au

British Embassy and Consulate Ploutárhou 1, 106 75 Athens; tel: 210 72 72 600, http://ukingreece.fco.gov.uk/en/

Canadian Embassy Ethnikis Antistaseos 48, 152 31 Athens; tel: 210 72 73 400, www.canadainternational.gc.ca/greece-grece

Irish Embassy Vassiléos Konstandínou 7, 106 74 Athens; tel: 210 72 32 771, www.dfa.ie/irish-embassy/greece

New Zealand General Consulate Kifisías 76, 115 26 Athens, tel: 210 69 24 136

South African Embassy and Consulate Kifisías 60, 151 25 Maroúsi, Athens; tel: 210 61 78 020
US Embassy and Consulate Vassilísis Sofías 91, 101 60 Athens; tel: 210 72 12 951; http://athens.usembassy.gov

EMERGENCIES

Police emergency Tel: **100**
Tourist police Tel: **171**
Fire Tel: **199**
Ambulance Tel: **166**

G

GAY AND LESBIAN TRAVELLERS

Greece is a very conservative country where traditional family relationships form the backbone of society. However, there is a natural courtesy towards visitors and this combined with all the different types of international tourist makes Athens a good destination for gay and lesbian travellers. There are gay-friendly bars, cafés and restaurants in the districts of Makrigiánni (south of the Acropolis), Gázi, Metaxourgío and Roúf (around Kerameikos) as well as Exárhia (near Omónia). Check gay events, news and locations at www.gayguide.gr.

GETTING THERE

By air. At present, Greece has two internationally active airlines, of which Olympic Air (www.olympicair.com) has flights to several UK destinations. Aegean Airlines (www.aegeanair.com) has flights from London Heathrow to Athens.
From the UK, British Airways (www.ba.com) offers daily direct services to Athens from London Heathrow; easyJet (www.easyjet.com) flies from London Gatwick and many other UK destinations. From Ireland, Aer Lingus (www.aerlingus.com) flies thrice weekly (May–Sept) from Dublin to Athens direct.

From North America, Delta (www.delta.com) flies directly to Athens from New York JFK year-round; Continental Airlines (www.continental.com) flies Newark–Athens direct seasonally, while American Airlines (www.aa.com) does Philadelphia–Athens May–Oct. Otherwise you'll arrive indirectly via a European hub on such airlines as Lufthansa (www.lufthansa.com), KLM (www.klm.com), British Airways (www.ba.com) or Alitalia (www.alitalia.com). There are no direct flights from either Australia or New Zealand to Athens; the most likely providers of advantageous multi-stop flights include Gulf Air (www.gulfair.com), Emirates (www.emirates.com), Singapore Airlines (www.singaporeair.com) and Thai Airlines (www.thaiairways.com).

By car. The all-overland route to Greece from western Europe goes via Austria, Hungary, Serbia and FYROM, with motorway conditions in FYROM leaving much to be desired. However, you can instead drive to the Italian ports of Venice, Ancona, Brindisi or Bari and take an overnight ferry to Igoumenítsa or Pátra on the Greek mainland. It is then a three-hour drive to Athens. The following companies currently offer trans-Adriatic service between Italy and Greece:

Agoudimos www.ferries.gr/agoudimos

ANEK www.anek.gr

Minoan Lines www.minoan.gr

Superfast www.superfast.com

Ventouris www.ventouris.gr

By rail. The train journey from the UK to Athens is expensive and takes three days; it is not possible to buy a through fare from the UK or Ireland to Greece in any case. Rail services from western Europe can link with the ferries at Ancona or Brindisi for onward sailing to Pátra and rail transfer to Athens. It only really makes sense to arrive by train if you're on a longer tour of many European countries. In the UK, contact **Voyages-SNCF** (https://uk.voyages-sncf.com/en) for discounted youth rail fares and InterRail passes.

GUIDES AND TOURS

Only officially certified guides may conduct tours of archaeological sites. You will find official guides at the entrance to the Acropolis, or you can book a personal guide through the nearby Greek National Tourist Organisation (EOT) office on Dionysíou Areopagítou.

There is ample choice if you want to book a guided group tour of Athens; however, walking tours are preferable to coach tours, which are likely to spend much of their time stalled in dense traffic. A coach tour is of most use for visiting Delphi, which is somewhat complicated to reach by public transport. Hotel reception desks are happy to arrange land tours for you, with pick-up/drop-off at the hotel.

'Three-islands-in-one-day' cruises of the Saronic Gulf are best avoided, allowing little time at each island. With a careful eye to hydrofoil or catamaran schedules, you can construct your own more leisurely itinerary taking in at least two islands.

H

HEALTH AND MEDICAL CARE

In case of medical emergency, **dial 166** (Greek) for an ambulance or to find the nearest open hospital. Emergency treatment is given free at public hospital casualty wards *(epígonda peristatiká)*. EU residents can

Where's the nearest (all-night) pharmacy? **Pou íne to kondinótero (dianikterévon) farmakío?**
I need a doctor/dentist **Hriázome éna giatró/odontogiatró**
an ambulance **éna asthenofóro**
a hospital **nosokomío**
I have... **Écho...**
a headache **ponokéfalo**
a fever **pyretós**
an upset stomach **anakatoméno stomáhi**
sunstroke **ilíasi**

get further theoretically free treatment (in practice there are small 'appointment fees' and outright bribes), but must carry a European Health Insurance Card (EHIC; tel: 0845 6062030 in the UK; www.ehic.org.uk to get one). It is advisable to take out additional travel insurance to cover you for protracted private treatment or repatriation.

If you are taking any medication, bring enough for your holiday needs and keep it in its original packaging. If you have a basic medical need, look for a chemist, or *farmakío*, signified by a green cross, where you may obtain advice. Most pharmacists speak some English.

Athens tap water is safe to drink, though bottled spring water is universally available.

L

LANGUAGE

Don't worry if you can't speak Greek. Most people working anywhere near the tourist industry will have a basic English vocabulary and many speak English very well. Both the *Berlitz Greek Phrase Book* and CD, or *Earworms Rapid Greek* volumes, cover nearly all situations you are likely to encounter.

In central Athens most street signs are dually marked in Greek and Latin alphabets, and lots of tourist information (including taverna menus) is given in (often idiosyncratic) English. The table below lists the Greek letters in their upper- and lower-case forms, followed by the closest individual or combined letters to which they correspond in English.

Α	α	a	as in bar
Β	β	v	as in veto
Γ	γ	g	as in go (except before 'i' and 'e' sounds, when it's like the y in yes)
Δ	δ	d	like th in 'this'
Ε	ε	e	as in get

Z	ζ	z	as in English
H	η	i	as in ski
Θ	θ	th	as in thin
I	ι	i l	as in ski
K	κ	k	as in English
Λ	λ	l	as in English
M	μ	m	as in English
N	ν	n	as in English
Ξ	ξ	x	as in box
O	o	o	as in road
Π	π	p	as in English
P	ρ	r	as in English
Σ	σ, ς	s	as in kiss, except like z before m or g sounds
T	τ	t	as in English
Y	υ	y	as in country
Φ	φ	f	as in English
X	χ	ch	as in Scottish loch
Ψ	ψ	ps	as in tipsy
O/Ω	ω	o	as in toad
AI	αι	e	as in hay
AY	αυ	av	as in avant-garde
EI	ει	i	as in ski
EY	ευ	ev	as in ever
OI	οι	i	as in ski
OY	ου	ou	as in soup
ΓΓ	γγ	ng	as in longer
ΓK	γκ	g	as in gone
ΓΞ	γξ	nx	as in anxious
MΠ	μπ	b or mb	as in beg or compass
NT	ντ	d or nd	as in dog or under

M

MAPS

The Greek Tourist Office produces a folding street map to aid your exploration of central Athens and Piraeus. Insight Fleximap Athens also provides full mapping, with all top attractions listed, and an easy-to-fold, laminated finish.

MEDIA

Radio. Athens International Radio at 104.4FM broadcasts in English much of the day, often transmitting material from the BBC World Service.
Press. Numerous English-language newspapers (US and UK) are available at newsstands. The *International Herald Tribune* appears daily and includes as a bonus the English-language version of top local paper *Kathimerini* (www.ekathimerini.com) The *Athens News* is published every Friday (but daily updates on www.athensnews.com) and has events listings and a TV guide. Bi-monthly *Odyssey* magazine (www.odyssey.gr) has interesting features and book reviews, plus social/political commentary.

MONEY

Currency. For the time being, the euro (€) is used in Greece. Notes of 100 euros and above are regarded with suspicion, as counterfeit, and can often only be broken down in banks.
Currency exchange. Most banks (Mon–Thu 8am–2.30pm, Fri 8am–2pm) exchange foreign currency notes but charge a commission (usually 1–3 percent). Exchange rates appear on a digital display, and are generally the same for each bank.

You can also change money at bureaux de change around Sýndagma, open longer hours than banks. Some advertise commission-free transactions, but exchange rates are often inferior to those of banks.
Automatic teller machines (ATMs). These are ubiquitous in central Athens, and the most convenient way to get euros.
Credit cards. Many hotels, car-hire companies, airline or ferry agencies and shops accept credit cards, though some make an additional

charge to cover their bank costs. Only the more expensive tavernas and restaurants are likely to accept cards.

> I want to change some pounds/dollars. **Thélo na alláxo merikés líres/meriká dollária.**
> How much commission do you take? **Póso promythia pérnete?**
> Can I pay with this credit card? **Boró na pliróso me avtí tin pistotikí kárta?**

O

OPENING TIMES

Most shops open Mon, Wed and Sat 9am–2.30pm, closing at 2pm on Tue, Thu and Fri but open additionally 5.30–8.30pm. However, tourist shops – in Pláka especially – will stay open seven days a week from 9am–10.30pm. Supermarkets open 9am–9pm Mon–Fri, 9am–8pm Sat; a very few work 10am–4pm Sun.

Museums and archaeological sites have unstable hours which may not match those given in the text; do not assume you can gain admission anywhere except Tue–Sun 9am– 2.30pm. The last admission is usually 20 minutes before closing.

P

POLICE (see also Complaints and Crime & safety)

Athens regular police wear two-tone uniforms, with steel-blue slacks and caps and powder-blue shirts, with a steel-blue jacket added in winter – except when on anti-riot duty. **Tourist police** (contact details under 'Complaints') have an additional white band on the cap and a white belt. These officers can speak English and act as interpreters should your case need to involve the main police force.

Where's the nearest police station? **Pou íne to kondinótero astynomikó tmíma?**

POST OFFICES

Post offices (open 7.30am–2pm) have blue-and-yellow livery, and are marked 'Elliniká Takhydromía' in Greek plus 'Hellenic Post' in English, with a stylised Hermes head as the logo. Stamps can be bought here and at substations (usually stationery shops).

Where's the (nearest) post office? **Pou íne to kondinótero tahydromío?**
A stamp for this letter/postcard, please. **Éna grammatósimo giaftó to grámma/giaftí tin kárta, parakaló.**
express/registered **katepígon/sistiméno**

PUBLIC HOLIDAYS

National official holidays fall on the following dates:
1 January New Year's Day *(Protohroniá)*
6 January Epiphany *(Theofánia)*
25 March Greek Independence/Annunciation *(Evangelismós)* Day
1 May May Day *(Protomagiá)*
15 August Dormition *(Kímisis)* of the Virgin
28 October National Ohi ('No') Day
25 December Christmas *(Hristoúgena)*
26 December *Sýnaxis tis Panagías* (Gathering of the Virgin's Entourage)
Moveable dates. The most important holiday in the Greek Orthodox calendar is Greek Orthodox Easter, which in some years coincides with the 'Western' (ie Catholic/Protestant) Easter, and other years falls a week or two to either side of it – in fact anything up to four weeks. It is advisable to

check the Easter dates (easiest on http://5ko.free.fr/en/easter.php) before booking a spring holiday as all services, especially flights, experience disruption at this time.

Moveable dates relative to Easter Sunday, all of them official holidays except Ascension Day, are the first day of Lent (Clean Monday; 48 days before Easter), Good Friday, Easter Monday, the Ascension (*Análipsi*; 39 days after Easter) and Pentecost (Whit Monday, Ágion Pnévma; 50 days after Easter).

T

TELEPHONES

The international code for Greece is 30. Within Greece, all phone numbers have 10 digits; fixed lines begin with 2, mobiles with 6.

Foreign visitors with tri-band mobiles can roam on any Greek network.

TIME ZONES

Greece is two hours ahead of Greenwich Mean Time and observes Daylight Savings along with the rest of Europe.

New York	London	**Athens**	Sydney	Auckland
5am	10am	**noon**	7pm	9pm

TIPPING

Service is notionally included in restaurant and bar bills although it is customary to leave between five and ten percent of the bill in small change on the table. In the week before Easter and at Christmas restaurants add an extra 'bonus' to the bill for the waiters.

TOILETS

All major tourist attractions have good facilities. Note that in many establishments toilet paper is still disposed of in the bin due to narrow drains.

Where are the toilets? **Pou íne ta apohoritíria?**

TOURIST INFORMATION

The **Greek National Tourist Organisation**, or Ellinikós Organismós Tourismoú (EOT; www.visitgreece.gr), is responsible for producing and dispersing tourist information. The EOT information office in Athens is conveniently sited in a purpose-built cabana at Dionysíou Areopagítou 18–20 (Mon–Fri 9am–5pm, Sat 10am–4pm; tel: 210 33 10 392).

UK and Ireland: 4 Great Portland Street, London, W1W 8QJ; tel: (020) 7495 9300.

US and Canada: 800 3rd Avenue, New York, NY 10022; tel: (212) 421 5777.

TRANSPORT

Metro. The Athens metro is clean, fast and glitch-free, and generally the best way to get around. The old, pre-2001 metro (Line 1), called ISAP, runs from Piraeus to Kifissiá. Line 2 runs between Ágios Dimítrios and Ágios Andónios. Line 3 runs between Agia Marina and Doukíssis Plakendías, with two special cars per hour, clearly marked, continuing beyond to the airport. Line 1 operates 5.30am–12.30am, lines 2 and 3 5.30am–12.30am on Sun–Thu and until 2am on Fri–Sat.

Buses and trams. An extensive bus network connects most places that the metro doesn't reach. Regular city buses run from 5am–midnight every 15–20 minutes per route. They can be crowded, so for short journeys it may be easier to walk or get a taxi. Tickets can be purchased individually or in bundles of 10 from news kiosks and special booths at both bus-route start-points. Augmenting the blue-and-white buses are yellow electric trolley buses.

The tramway (Sun–Thu 5.30am–1am, Fri–Sat until 2.30am) operates routes from Sýndagma down to Voúla and to Néo Fáliro's Peace and Friendship Stadium ('SEF' on electronic car displays), with a link between the latter two points.

Fares, tickets and updates. A single ticket for a metro, bus or tram costs €1.40 and is valid for 90 minutes after validation, allowing transfers between the three systems. A 24-hour ticket valid for all means of transport costs €4.50, while a 5-day pass is €9. Tickets are best purchased at metro stations, either from coin-op machines or an attended window. Fines for fare-dodging are a stiff 60 times the amount of the single fare evaded; rules are complicated and changeable, so unwitting violations occur. The main hazards for newcomers are attempting to switch from airport express bus to metro (not allowed) or forgetting to validate tickets. In 2017, Athens paper tickets will be changed to plastic smartcards so check for updates at www.athenstransport.com.

The Athens Urban Transport Organisation (OASA; www.oasa.gr) issues a free transport map. This can be obtained from metro stations or from the OASA office at Metsóvou 15. Consult the website for fare updates.

Taxis. Taxis, painted yellow and with a TAXI sign atop the vehicle and on the side, are numerous and affordable. Meters are set to €1.29 at the start of each journey, with a minimum fare of €3.44; the '1' indicates regular fare, '2' indicates double tariff between midnight and 5am, or beyond urban areas. Taxi drivers are fine to round up to the nearest euro. Tariff rules appear on a laminated sheet mounted on the dashboard. In the city you can hail taxis in the street, but extra-long or short distances may be unpopular with drivers. All hotels will call a taxi for you for pick-up at reception. Fare-fiddling is not unknown, so the following sample '1' charges are useful: short hop across the centre, €5–8; city centre to Piraeus, €15; city centre to the airport, €38 including airport surcharge, tolls and baggage. Phoning for a taxi attracts a surcharge, and luggage in the boot costs €0.43 per item.

Ferries, catamarans, hydrofoils. Daily services operate to all nearby islands, from Piraeus to the Saronic Gulf and the Cyclades, and from Rafína to the Cyclades. For details contact Piraeus Port Police (tel: 210 42 26 000) or Rafína Port Police (tel: 22940 22300) – however, English is unlikely to be spoken on the outgoing recorded messages. With internet access, it's better to check the website of Hellenic Seaways (www.hellenicseaways.gr), which handles all sailings to Póros, Ýdra and Spétses. For Égina, the following alternatives are also available: Nova Ferries (www.novaferries.gr), the Agios Nektarios (www.anes.gr) and Aegean Flying Dolphins (www.aegeanflyingdolphins.gr).

VISAS AND ENTRY REQUIREMENTS

European Union (EU) citizens may enter Greece for an unlimited length of time. British citizens must have a valid passport. Citizens of Ireland can enter with a valid identity card or passport. Citizens of the US, Canada, Australia and New Zealand can stay for up to 90 days within any 180-day period upon production of a valid passport; no advance visas are needed, but extensions of the basic tourist stamp are almost impossible to obtain – you must leave the Schengen Zone for at least 90 days before re-entry.

WEBSITES

Websites for useful organisations have been included throughout this guide; however, the following general websites are also helpful:
www.meteo.gr five-day advance forecasts, with many reporting stations
www.culture.gr the Ministry of Culture home-page; English option
www.athensguide.com the Athens page of Matt Barrett's acclaimed general Greek website.

YOUTH HOSTELS

The following are currently two of the better, most central student hostels in Athens, but go to www.hostelworld.com for more choice:
Athens Backpackers, Makrí 12, tel: 210 92 24 044.
Student and Traveller's Inn, Kydathinéon 16, tel: 210 32 44 808.

RECOMMENDED HOTELS

Hotels were formerly classified in six categories – Luxury, A, B, C, D and E – but recently this system has been replaced with analogous star ratings, from five down to none. Room rates for all categories other than five star/luxury are government-controlled. Categories are determined by the common facilities at the hotel, not by the quality of the rooms. Thus, a three-star/B-class hotel room may be just as comfortable as a five-star/luxury hotel room, but will not have a conference room, swimming pool and so on. All two-star/C-class hotels are en suite, clean and reasonably furnished, and should provide breakfast. One-star/D-class hotels must be en suite but will usually have little else on offer; no-star/E-class are effectively extinct in Athens.

Tax and service charges should be included in quoted rates, though breakfast (typically €6–12 per person) may not be – check. The prices ranges below are for a double room per night in high season.

€€€€€	over 250 euros
€€€€	180–250 euros
€€€	120–180 euros
€€	70–120 euros
€	below 70 euros

MAKRYGIÁNNI AND VEÍKOU

Acropolis Select €€ *Falírou 37–39, 117 42 Athens, metro Acropolis, tel: 210 92 11 610, www.acropoliselect.gr.* A six-storey hotel with helpful staff and a reasonable location. It has a pleasant if dark-toned lounge-bar, a plush breakfast area/restaurant with skylight, off-street parking, and wi-fi access for an hourly fee, but no roof garden. Some rooms have Acropolis views. 72 rooms.

Art Gallery €–€€ *Erekhthíou 5, 117 42 Athens, metro Syngroú-Fix, tel: 210 92 38 376, www.artgalleryhotel.gr.* This small pension-hotel, named after the artwork on the walls of the common areas, has assorted parquet-floored rooms, with family-sized suites on the roof. Note that some rooms have their bathrooms in the hallway. Pleasant breakfast bar on the terrace with Acropolis views. 22 rooms.

Hera €€€ *Falírou 9, 117 42 Athens, metro Acropolis, tel: 210 923 6682,* www.herahotel.gr. The Hera has perhaps the best roof garden in the area, with a heated bar-restaurant for all-year operation. Rooms are on the small side, so it's worth paying extra for three fifth-floor suites with bigger balconies (some fourth-floor rooms also have Acropolis views). The dome-lit atrium-breakfast room, and friendly staff, are further assets. 38 rooms.

Herodion €€€€ *Rovértou Gálli 4, 117 42 Athens, metro Acropolis, tel: 210 92 36 832,* www.herodion.gr. The Herodion scores most points for its common areas: the café-restaurant with conservatory seating shaded by wild pistachios, a small business corner, and the roof garden with two Jacuzzi tubs and eyefuls of the Acropolis. Functional but fair-sized rooms, some with Acropolis views. 86 rooms, 4 suites.

Marble House € *Alley off Anastasíou Zínni 35, 117 41 Athens, metro Syngroú-Fix, tel: 210 92 28 294,* www.marblehouse.gr. This welcoming, family-run pension has an enviably quiet location. All rooms have balconies, baths, fridges, air con and free wi-fi. Great value – book well in advance. 16 rooms. Credit cards for deposit only.

PLÁKA

Acropolis House €–€€ *Kódrou 6–8, 105 57 Athens, metro Sýndagma, tel: 210 32 22 344,* www.acropolishouse.gr. The first neoclassical mansion in Athens to be converted into a pension. The building's listed status prevents some of it rooms having en suite baths, though for the academic clientele that's part of the charm, and it is well kept. All rooms have solid wood floors, most have high ceilings (some with murals). Communal fridge and two breakfast rooms. 19 rooms. Cash preferred.

Ava €€€€–€€€€€ *Lysikrátous 9–11, 105 58 Athens, tel: 210 32 59 000,* www.avahotel.gr. Suite-format hotel, thoroughly overhauled to the highest standards in 2016. Upper units have balconies with courtyard, or oblique Acropolis views. Excellent for families as they are roomier (up to 55 square metres) units, effectively 1-bedroom apartments, which comfortably fit four. There are also smaller suites suitable for couples. Breakfast included, wi-fi throughout, assiduous service.

Electra Palace €€€€ *Navárhou Nikodímou 18–20, 105 57 Athens, tel: 210 33 70 000*, www.electrahotels.gr. The only real luxury outfit in Pláka, the neoclassical Electra Palace is an oasis, with a small pool and pleasant spa in the basement, and a lawn garden. Luxury suites have dark wood floors, oriental rugs and Jacuzzis. A newer wing with a rooftop pool perches above the parking garage (fee). 155 rooms.

Hermes €€€ *Apóllonos 19, 105 57 Athens, metro Sýndagma, tel: 210 32 35 514*, www.hermeshotel.gr. Part of a family-run chain, the Hermes has a breakfast room on the mezzanine, decorated with manager Dorína Stathopoúlou's professional photographs. The street-level lounge-bar is naturally lit by a light well. Front-facing rooms are smaller but have balconies; all rooms were renovated in 2016 and have marble baths. 45 rooms.

New €€€ *Fillelínon 16, metro Sýndagma, 105 57 Athens, tel: 210 32 73 000*, www.yeshotels.gr. Nearly four years in the making, this design hotel, opened in 2011, is a collaboration between a team of Greek architecture students and the celebrated Brazilian brothers Fernando and Humberto Campana. The wooden furniture of the site's previous, undistinguished hotel has been fragmented and ingeniously incorporated as installations in the communal areas alongside contemporary elements. Rooms are equally quirky without being in-your-face; breakfast and service are excellent. The only black mark is the traffic noise – try for a room facing quieter Navárhou Nikodímou. 79 rooms.

Phaedra € *Herefóndos 16, corner Adrianoú, 105 58 Athens, metro Acropolis, tel: 210 32 38 461*, www.hotelphaedra.com. The Phaedra offers the best budget value in Pláka. Not all rooms are en suite, but some have balconies looking onto the square with its Byzantine church. Breakfast is served in a pleasant ground-floor salon. 21 rooms.

MONASTIRÁKI AND PSYRRÍ

Arion €€€ *Agíou Dimitríou 18, 105 54 Athens, metro Monastiráki, tel: 210 32 40 415*, www.arionhotel.gr. This hotel in the heart of Pysrrí has spacious Japanese-accented rooms with lattice closet doors, modular headboards, square light fittings, but no balconies (though there is a roof terrace for all). Quiet despite its proximity to *ouzerís* and bars. 51 rooms.

Attalos €€ *Athinás 29, 105 54 Athens, metro Monastiráki, tel: 210 32 12 801*, www.attaloshotel.com. This friendly hotel is good value and retains many of its period features, but medium-sized rooms themselves – about half with balconies, costing a tad more – have modern furnishings, double glazing against street noise, parquet floors and pastel/earth tones. Facilities include free wi-fi and a very popular if somewhat cramped roof-terrace bar operating from 6.30pm onwards. 78 rooms.

Carolina € *Kolokotróni 55, 105 60 Athens, metro Monastiráki, tel: 210 32 43 551*, www.hotelcarolina.gr. The Carolina offers the best value locally for airy, white-tile rooms and large included breakfasts. The best – if potentially hottest – rooms are the fifth-floor 'retirées' up on the roof, with shade from a wooden awning out front; all others have balconies (sometimes two), and the rear-facing units have limited Acropolis views. 33 rooms.

Cecil € *Athinás 39, 105 54 Athens, tel: 210 32 17 079*, www.cecil.gr. This well-restored 1850s vintage mansion has some great period features such as its iron-cage elevator. For conservation reasons, rooms have no balconies – unless you count the ornamental ones out front – but they offer parquet floors, iron bedsteads, double glazing, pastel colours, retiled baths and free wi-fi. Breakfast served on first floor. 39 rooms.

OMÓNIA

Art €€ *Márni 27, 104 32 Athens, metro Omónia, tel: 210 52 40 501*, www.arthotelathens.gr. Set in an interwar Art Nouveau/neoclassical building, the Art offers one-of-a-kind rooms. Bathrooms are also unique, most with chrome washbasins. Common areas include a basement events hall and stunning reception atrium with a circular light well. Keen pricing reflects the less than desirable area, though you are close to the Archaeological Museum. 30 rooms.

Fresh €€€ *Sofokléous 26, corner Klisthénous, 105 52 Athens, metro Omónia, tel: 210 52 48 511,* www.freshhotel.gr. You will either love or hate this startling 'design' hotel, with its lollipop colour scheme of panels everywhere from reception to the balconies. Chrome, leather and glass abound, but there is also plenty of oak and walnut. Modern room features include bedside remote control of windows and plasma TV. The rooftop pool-and-bar is a big hit and the six superior rooms have private Zen rock gardens. 133 rooms.

Pallas Athena €€ *Athinás 65, 105 51 Athens, metro Omónia, tel: 210 32 50 900,* www.grecotelpallasathena.com. One of the quirkier boutique hotels in Athens. The reception desks sit on Mini Cooper cars; the 'graffiti' rooms are decorated by local artists. Rooms vary; some have views to Platía Kotziá, some have balconies, though all have spacious baths and free wi-fi. 63 rooms.

SÝNDAGMA

Grande Bretagne €€€€€ *Platía Syndágmatos, metro Sýndagma, tel: 210 33 30 000,* www.grandebretagne.gr. Perhaps the most famous hotel in Athens, oozing history and class, the Grande Bretagne on Sýndagma Square dates from 1846. A 2006 renovation restored every period detail to its belle époque glory, with 'Deluxe' doubles comparable to junior suites elsewhere. Sumptuous communal areas include a landscaped pool garden, a ballroom, plus a basement spa with a palm court, and large pool, hamam and sauna. 320 rooms.

King George Palace €€€€€ *Platía Syndágmatos, metro Sýndagma, tel: 210 32 22 210,* www.kinggeorgeathens.com. The King George Palace is a more intimate, scaled-down version of the Grande Bretagne. It has the same Second Empire furnishings, which jar a bit with the flat-screen TVs, recessed lighting and sound systems. Bathrooms are palatial, with marble trim. Actively pitched at a business clientele, with a functions room, gym and spa. 102 rooms and suites.

KOLONÁKI

St George Lycabettus €€€–€€€€ *Kleoménous 2, 106 75 Athens, metro Evangelismós, tel: 210 72 90 711,* www.sglycabettus.gr. 2016-renovated hotel at the foot of Mount Lykavittós (Lycabettus). Room decor varies from luridly plush to minimalist; all have wi-fi access, the most covetable looking over the city. Facilities include Jacuzzi, sauna, massage studio, gym and roof pool, as well as an in-house art gallery. 134 rooms, 20 suites.

Periscope €€€€–€€€€€ *Háritos 22, 106 75 Athens, metro Evangelismós, tel: 210 72 97 200,* www.periscope.gr. Slick hotel with arresting black-, white- and grey-toned rooms; the higher you are in the building, the better the units, culminating in airy balconied suites, and a rooftop Jacuzzi. All units have wood floors, flat-screen TVs and music systems. And yes, there is a rooftop periscope scanning the skyline, with images projected down to the handy ground-floor bistro. 21 units.

AMBELÓKIPI (PLATÍA MAVÍLI)

Airotel Alexandros €€ *Timoléondos Vássou 8, 115 21 Athens, metro Ambelókipi, tel: 210 64 30 464,* www.airotel.gr. On a little square behind a chapel, the Airotel Alexandros offers decent accommodation behind a slightly forbidding exterior. The high-ceilinged lounge is flanked by the brick-and-pastel-panelled restaurant. 82 rooms, 11 suites.

Embassy €€–€€€ *Timoléondos Vássou 22, 115 21 Athens, metro Ambelókipi, tel: 210 64 15 000,* www.embassyhotel.gr. Formerly the Andromeda, this businessmen's hotel became the Embassy in 2010, with a full makeover. Modern room decor, with veneer floors and bathrooms with steel sinks, features blue, grey and white hues (except for the junior suite in earth tones). Rear units have balconies with a leafy view, though front rooms are bigger, with round dining tables. All have trouser presses and coffee/tea machines. Common areas are restricted to the ground-floor bar and breakfast area. 22 rooms, 9 suites.

ARGOLID PENINSULA

La Belle Hélène € *Main road, Mykínes 212 00 (Mycenae), tel: 27510 76225.* This 1862-built house retains its Victorian ambience – you can even sleep in the bed Heinrich Schliemann used during his excavations at Mycenae. Conservation rules mean bathrooms are not en suite, but the hospitality is excellent. The guestbook has signatures of the famous (e.g. Agatha Christie, Virginia Woolf) and infamous (assorted Nazi brass). 5 rooms. Cash only.

Candia House €€–€€€ *211 00 Kándia Iríon, tel: 27520 94060,* www.candia house.gr. A small hotel owned by a delightful Athenian who wanted to create a peaceful haven for her guests. On a sandy beach 17km (11 miles) southeast of Náfplio, it is ideally placed for touring the area. The individually designed suites have living rooms, kitchens and balconies. Facilities include a pool, gym and sauna. Open May–Oct. 10 suites.

Marianna €€€ *Potamianoú 9, 211 00 Náfplio, tel: 27520 24265,* www.hotel marianna.gr. Restored and run by three hospitable brothers, this boutique hotel nestles against Akronafplía fortress's rocky walls, its patios planted with orange trees. Rooms, some with exposed masonry, are attractive and comfortable. Delicious home-made breakfasts are served on a raised terrace with fabulous views over the old town and the bay. 21 rooms.

SARONIC GULF ISLANDS

Bratsera €€–€€€ *180 40 Ýdra (Hydra), tel: 22980 53971,* www.bratsera hotel.com. This hotel occupies a former sponge factory, and the extensive common areas (including a conference room and Ýdra's only pool) double as a museum of the industry, with photos and artefacts. Large rooms, in six grades, have flagstone floors and showers. Open late March–end Oct. 25 rooms.

Brown €€ *Southern waterfront, past Panagítsa church, 180 10 Égina, tel: 22970 22271,* www.hotelbrown.gr. Égina town's top hotel, facing the southerly beach, occupying a former sponge factory dating from 1886.

The best and calmest units are the garden bungalows at the rear; there are also galleried family suites sleeping four. 28 units.

Economou Mansion €€€€ *Kounoupítsa district, 400m/yds from Dápia port, 180 50 Spétses,* tel: 22980 73400, www.economouspetses.gr. Spetses' premier restoration inn is part of an 1851-vintage property. The ground floor of the main house has six well-converted rooms with ample period features; a newer outbuilding hosts two luxury sea-view suites. Breakfast served by the pool. 8 units. Cash only.

Eginitiko Arhontiko € *corner Thomaïdou and Ayíou Nikoláou, 180 10 Égina,* tel: 22970 24156, www.aeginitikoarchontiko.gr. A late 18th-century neoclassical mansion, now converted into a small hotel with well-appointed rooms. The *pièce de résistance* is the suite with painted ceilings. There is also a breakfast conservatory with coloured glass windows. 12 rooms. Cash only.

Pavlou €€ *Megálo Neório Beach, Kalávria, Póros,* tel: 22980 22734, www.pavlouhotel.gr. Family-run, family-pitched hotel just behind one of the better island beaches, with pool, tennis court and restaurant. Rooms have contemporary furnishings, with about half having sea-view balconies. Open May–Oct. 36 rooms.

DELPHI AREA

Ganimede/Ganymidis €€ *Nikoláou Gourgoúri 20 (southwest market street), 330 52 Galaxídi,* tel: 22650 41328, www.ganimede.gr. This restoration hotel in an historic port south of Delphi is superbly managed by the Papalexis family. There are six doubles in the old ship-captain's mansion, remoter studios, and a family suite across the courtyard garden where a copious breakfast is served, featuring exquisite homemade pâtés and jams. Booking essential, especially weekends year-round.

Pan € *Pávlou ké Frederíkis 53, 330 54 Delfí,* tel: 22650 82294, www.panartemis.gr. Comfortable, excellent-value hotel with fine views of the gulf. Its *Artemis* annexe opposite has doubles equal in standard to the family quads of the Pan, but lacking the sea views. 21 rooms total.

INDEX

Acropolis 29
  Beule Gate 31
  Erechtheion 36
  New Acropolis
    Museum 39
  Nike temple 31
  Old Temple of Athena
    37
  Parthenon 34
  Porch of the Caryatids
    36
  Propylaea 32
  Sanctuary of Artemis
    Brauronia 34
Agía Iríni 57
Ágii Apóstoli 48
Ágios Dimítrios
  Lombardiáris 41
Altar of Ares 48
Anafiótika 43
Aráhova 80
Areopagos Hill 42
Argolid Peninsula 74
Athens and Epidauros
  Festival 39, 80
Benaki Museum 66
Benaki Museum Collection
  of Islamic Art 54
Benaki Museum Pireós
  Annexe 56
Bouleuterion 52
Brauron 70
Byzantine and Christian
  Museum 67
Corinth 75
  Acrocorinth 77
  Ancient Corinth 77
  Bema 77
  Corinth Canal 75
  Fountain of Peirene 77
  Temple of Apollo 77

Delphi 81
Égina 72
  Agía Marína 72
  Temple of Aphaea 72
Eleusis 69
Exárhia 62
Fethiye Tzami 46
Frissiras Museum 43
Galaxídi 80
Gázi 56
Greek Agora 47
Hadrian's Arch 64
Hadrian's Library 53
Hephaisteion 50
Herakleidon 54
Hill of the Nymphs 42
Hill of the Pnyx 41
Jewish Museum of
  Greece 44
Kallimármaro Stadium 65
Kanellopoulos Museum 45
Kapnikaréa 53
Kerameikos 55
Little Asia 57
Man and Tools 45
Metroön 52
Mikrí Mitrópolis 45
Mitrópolis 45
monastery of Dafní 68
monastery of Kessarianí 68
Monastiráki Square 53
Monument of Filopappos
  40
Monument to Lysikratos 44
Mount Parnassós 80
Museum of Cycladic Art 66
Museum of Greek Folk
  Art and Greek Folk
  Music Instruments 53
Museum of the City of
  Athens 60

Mycenae 78
National Academy 61
National Archaeological
  Museum 58
National Gallery 67
National Gardens 64
National Historical
  Museum 60
National Library 61
Návplio 80
  Archaeological
    Museum 81
  Boúrtzi 81
  Peloponnesian
    Folklore
    Foundation 81
Nemea 77
New Bouleuterion 52
Numismatic Museum 62
Oberlander Museum 56
Odeion of Agrippa 48
Odeion of Herodes
  Atticus 38
Omónia Square 57
Panagía Pandánassa 53
Parliament Building 62
Piraeus 71
Pláka 43
Pompeion 56
Póros 73
  Monastery of
    Zoödóhou Pigís 73
  Poseidon temple 73
Psyrrí 53
Roman Forum 46
Sacred Gate 55
Sanctuary of Asklepion 80
Saronic Gulf Islands 72
Soúnio 70
Spétses 74
Stage of Phaedros 39

Stoa of Attalos 48
Sýndagma 62
Tekhnópolis 56
Temple of Ares 48
Temple of Olympian
    Zeus 64

Theatre of Dionysos 39
Theatre of Epidauros 79
Themistoklean Wall 41
Theoharakis Foundation
    for Fine Arts and
    Music 66

Tholos (Prytaneion) 51
Tzisdarákis Mosque 53
Varvákio 57
War Museum 67
Ydra 73
Záppeio 64

INSIGHT ⊙ GUIDES POCKET GUIDE

ATHENS

First Edition 2017

Editor: Helen Fanthorpe
Updaters: Magdalena Helsztyńska-Stadnik,
Marc Dubin
Head of Production: Rebeka Davies
Picture Editor: Tom Smyth
Cartography Update: Carte
Update Production: Apa Digital
Photography Credits: Andreas Prott/
iStockphoto 5TC; A Benaki Museum 4TC;
Britta Jaschinski/Apa Publications 87; Daniella
Nowitz/Apa Publications 5MC, 5M, 15, 20,
66; dejan suc/iStockphoto 75; Earl Eliason/
iStockphoto 73; Fratelli Alinari Museum of
the History of Photography, Florence 24;
Getty Images 4MC, 11, 12, 28; Glyn Genin/Apa
Publications 44, 52, 90; Greek National Tourism
Organisation 5M, 82, 85, 95; Grigorios Moraitis/
iStockphoto 19; iStock 7R, 33, 35, 36, 38, 49,
61, 63, 78, 81, 97; Klaas Lingbeek- van Kranen/
iStockphoto 42; Maarten Dirkse 4TL; Maria
Kutrakova/Fotolia 30; Ming Tang-Evans/Apa
Publications 99; Public domain 17, 69; Rebecca
Bizonet 46; Rebecca Erol/Apa Publications 6L,
102; Richard Nowitz/Apa Publications 4ML, 5T,
5MC, 6R, 23, 41, 57, 59, 76, 88; Roland Nagy 71;
Shutterstock 7, 55, 64; Simela Pantzartzi/Epa/
REX/Shutterstock 101; woe/Fotolia 50
Cover Picture: Shutterstock

Distribution
UK, Ireland and Europe: Apa Publications
(UK) Ltd; sales@insightguides.com
United States and Canada: Ingram Publisher
Services; ips@ingramcontent.com
Australia and New Zealand: Woodslane;
info@woodslane.com.au
Southeast Asia: Apa Publications (SN) Pte;
singaporeoffice@insightguides.com

Hong Kong, Taiwan and China:
Apa Publications (HK) Ltd;
hongkongoffice@insightguides.com
Worldwide: Apa Publications (UK) Ltd;
sales@insightguides.com

**Special Sales, Content Licensing
and CoPublishing**
Insight Guides can be purchased in bulk
quantities at discounted prices. We can
create special editions, personalised jackets
and corporate imprints tailored to your
needs. sales@insightguides.com;
www.insightguides.biz

Contact us
Every effort has been made to provide
accurate information in this publication,
but changes are inevitable. The publisher
cannot be responsible for any resulting loss,
inconvenience or injury. We would appreciate
it if readers would call our attention to any
errors or outdated information. We also
welcome your suggestions; please contact us
at: hello@insightguides.com
www.insightguides.com

Athens Metro

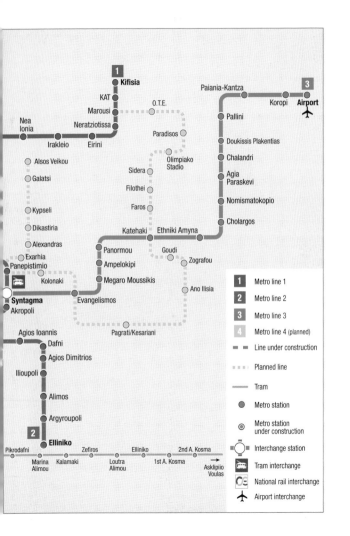

INSIGHT GUIDES

OFF THE SHELF

Since 1970, INSIGHT GUIDES has provided a unique perspective on the world's best travel destinations by using specially commissioned photography and illuminating text written by local authors.

Whether you're planning a city break, a walking tour or the journey of a lifetime, our superb range of guidebooks and phrasebooks will inspire you to discover more about your chosen destination.

INSIGHT GUIDES

offer a unique combination of stunning photos, absorbing narrative and detailed maps, providing all the inspiration and information you need.

PHRASEBOOKS & DICTIONARIES

help users to feel at home, when away. Pocket-sized with a free app to download, they go where you do.

CITY GUIDES

pack hundreds of great photos into a smaller format with detailed practical information, so you can navigate the world's top cities with confidence.

EXPLORE GUIDES

feature easy-to-follow walks and itineraries in the world's most exciting destinations, with our choice of the best places to eat and drink along the way.

POCKET GUIDES

combine concise information on where to go and what to do in a handy compact format, ideal on the ground. Includes a full-colour, fold-out map.

EXPERIENCE GUIDES

feature offbeat perspectives and secret gems for experienced travellers, with a collection of over 100 ideas for a memorable stay in a city.

www.insightguides.com